Terry Col'

Life and Love of Food

I sincerely hope you enjoy my story

Best wishes

Terry

By

Terence Clifford Colby

Copyright © 2024 Terence Clifford Colby

All rights reserved. No part of this publication may be reproduced, distributed, or transmitted in any form or by any means, including photocopying, recording, or other electronic or mechanical methods, without the author's prior written permission, including cover pictures, permitted by copyright law.

ISBN 9798883860651

Published by Amazon.

Cover picture – Terry holding a prime piece of beef forerib.

Dedication

To Jeannette, my golden girl!

Machins smokehouse 2023   Chris Bubb

1920 Gabriel Machin Butcher

Gabriel Machin Ltd., Butcher, and Poulterer was originally listed as a pub, then a greengrocer in the 1841 census. The first butcher to work there was Richard Blackall, recorded in the 1861 census, followed by Alfred Lester in 1871.

Gabriel Machin was born in Reading in 1836. He bought the business in 1881, living on-site with his wife Ellen and their children.

Ellen passed away in 1886, with Gabriel following her ten years later in 1896. Gabriel Junior, who was born in 1865, continued to run the family business until he died in 1933, after which his son Edward Norman took over.

The war and rationing were more than Edward could cope with, so he sold the shop in 1942 and took a job with the Ministry of Food as an area meat agent. When he sold the business, Edward stipulated that the Machin name had to remain over the shop.

In 1958, the Marett family came to manage the shop, however, it was owned by William Lee, who had a couple of other shops.

Colin Marett left school in 1962, aged 15, to work there too, following his family.

William Lee sold the business in 1965, and luckily Sidney and Lilian Marett purchased it.

Colin Marett became the owner in 1971, developing the business, and then selling it on to Ian Blandford in 2003.

Finally, Barry Wagner bought the shop from Ian Blandford in 2014. He is the current owner.

Contents

Chapter	Page
1 Early days, earliest inspirations	1
2 Growing pains	7
3 Kcab Gnals	17
4 Evolution	18
5 Wonderful fromage	24
6 Fishes La Mer	32
7 Christmas	43
8 Personalities	51
9 Creation	56
10 Environmental Health	63
11 Environment	65
12 To catch a thief!	70
13 All change	73
14 Terry 'Two Jobs'	78
15 Homecoming	82
16 Terry goes walkabout (Dagayu) Food discovery Through travel	85
17 'Two Jobs' continued	100
18 Homecoming (again)	107
A few of Terry's favourite recipes	114

Introduction

The seed of this book was sewn in my mum's kitchen as a young child, which grew slowly over the following 60-plus years with my insatiable quest to educate myself on food – all food!

On leaving school at fifteen my path had a real 'growth spurt' when I joined Gabriel Machin butcher's shop. My life skills started that day. I consider the years 1969 to 1998 my academy years! I learned so much during this time.

My thirst for knowledge was further satisfied by reading books written by foodies and artisans of the trade, or sometimes watching a skilled person create something extraordinary, whether in person or on TV.

Markets have been a useful source of information, particularly if the sellers produced the product. I once watched a butcher in France carve up a carcass. I noticed their cutting techniques were different from the way we do it in England. I thoroughly enjoyed the time I spent learning how they prepared the muscles.

Cheese is another obsession, another love of my life, even more than chocolate! Knowing and loving cheese has been a great asset, particularly to our customers over the years who I hope I've kept informed about new varieties and flavours.

I would love to work at Neal's Yard, as their cheese is superb. Their experience and expertise would've rubbed off on me, guaranteeing an expanded knowledge!

My kitchen skills have grown considerably. I now have profound respect for hard-working chefs, particularly Rick Stein, because he pays great attention to the quality of the ingredients he is using. He may not be the most skillful chef, but his passion for quality ingredients is second to none.

I may have retired, but my foodie interest never wanes. If I find a new cheese, I can't help but imagine stocking it in my cheese cabinet, or the discovery of an interesting meat product I would consider selling in my shop! However, Jeannette, my wife, does try to keep my feet on the ground by reminding me I am retired and I not starting any new business!

My son, Alex, has great skill and understanding of food, as he is similarly enthusiastic. I would've loved to see him follow a similar path in some capacity, however, the potential hours needed for this were understandably not attractive to him.

My stepson Mario is an amazing chef. We were at one time planning to go into business together, but that didn't materialise. He has gone on to own a restaurant, Mika in Abu Dhabi, which is continuing to develop and flourish very well.

I thoroughly enjoy cooking and would encourage everyone to prepare their meals; this gives you a greater appreciation and understanding of ingredients. Also, many supermarkets' 'ready meals' contain additives, creating a longer shelf life, however, they should be avoided if possible, so, cook for yourself, it is much healthier!

If you can grow some food, vegetables, and fruit yourself, that's even better; you don't need masses of room, and the little time spent will be worth it. You will be in control of how they mature. I have to say I am particularly disappointed with the organic movement, as all too often a section of the public uses it as a statement of wealth, rather than a healthy option.

Food produced in this country: meats, cheeses, grains and bread, etc., are an expression of the land where they're produced; the fruition of the farmers and artisans who created and grew these fabulous foods.

I sincerely hope you enjoy reading my book, and my journey of food exploration. If any part of it motivates the desire for further knowledge, then this has been more successful than I could have wished.

Terry Colby

Henley-on-Thames

Chapter 1

Early days, earliest inspirations

(Sowing the Seeds)

I was born and raised in Wargrave, a village on the Thames, just under four miles from Henley-on-Thames. My father, Clifford James Colby, was originally from Liverpool, however, his family moved to Wargrave after being bombed out of their homes during the Second World War in Liverpool, and then Portsmouth. A relative who worked at Wargrave Manor helped them find an empty cottage on the High Street, where they settled. My mother, Gladys, lived with her parents at Gibstroude Farm, owned by the Bush family in Crazies Hill. My parents had nine children, but sadly, one son died in a tragic accident before I was born. As a result, I grew up with six sisters and one brother, all of us living in a small cottage on the High Street that was once owned by Wargrave Manor.

My father worked as a Marine Engineer and electrician at Bushnell's, the local boatyard. My mum was a housewife, with no time for anything but to look after her large family. Mum was a good cook, and mealtimes must have been like feeding the troops, consequently, food was simple: fill them all up for a reasonable cost, lots of vegetables, and not much meat. My father was a very industrious worker, but never well paid, so I know times were often difficult for Mum.

Sunday was often Mum's baking day, which I loved. She baked wonderful sponge cakes and if I was lucky, I could clean out the mixing bowl afterwards. We'd spread Mum's homemade jam in the middle of the cakes, or a slice of cake with butter (or margarine) spread on top was heavenly! We all loved the fantastic puddings Mum made; bread and butter pudding, rice pudding, crumbles, and spotted dick, which Mum would steam in a muslin cloth.

The most amazing thing about Mum's cooking was that she instinctively knew the quantity of ingredients to use in everything she cooked or baked by 'eye', as she never had a set of scales to weigh anything.

When I was young, we kept chickens, and just occasionally Dad would wring one's neck, and then Mum would pluck it and roast it for dinner. I remember one occasion Dad had 'dispatched' a chicken, laying it on the table for Mum to deal with. Well, before she could do anything, the chicken jumped up and ran around the table two or three times then dropped down dead in an obvious last act of defiance!

Food shops in our village regularly attracted my attention, including Stringers, who sold fruit and vegetables. They had a sweet counter where I used to buy Wagon Wheels, sherbet dips, or sometimes a lucky bag, containing sherbet, liquorice, and toffees.

Budgens was another interesting shop. They sold bread, delicious looking cakes, and teas, and they would grind coffee beans, which gave the shop a wonderful aroma. The shop manager was Bill Newman, whom I later became friends with. We often played billiards at the local club.

The Colby Family

Sue, Carol, Terry, Jackie, Linda, Pam, Sheila, Dad (Clifford), Paul and Mum Gladys

We also had Jennings the butcher; I would lean on the windowsill outside, looking at the trays of meats within: mince, sausages, and chops below, with joints and chickens hanging above, overhead.

In my early teens, I had a Saturday job at Jennings, and rode his delivery bike all around the village, delivering meat parcels. One house I delivered to was in Borough Marsh where they had a dog who used to chase me, so I would race full pelt up their driveway, putting my feet up so the dog couldn't bite my ankles.

Peter Jennings, the owner, taught me how to 'bone out' sides of bacon - my introduction to butchery.

International Stores was another shop on the high street, a grocery where Mum would send me to buy ½ lb of ham, which always smelt wonderful. The lady in the shop would cut large cheeses with a wire, which I thought was amazing. We bought our biscuits there too; a big bag of broken biscuits, which were a mixture of all sorts from different biscuit producers. They came in a big chest; I think from Huntley and Palmers in Reading.

The shop that attracted me the most was Tony Shaw, the fishmonger, just over the road from our house. The window was full of silver trays laid out with all sorts of different fish: cod, herrings, kippers, yellow haddock, and others I'd never heard of; one had spots all over it. There were often hares hanging in the window with cups on their noses, which I later found out were there to catch the blood dripping out of them.

I was interested in the eggs they had for sale. Not just hen's eggs, but duck eggs, which were often a beautiful colour blue, or sometimes a pale shade of green. Occasionally there were huge goose eggs, but best of all were the gull eggs, which I found fascinating. Their colour variations of browns, beige, and greys, with amazing markings of blobs and dashes with no two eggs the same pattern, I thought they were beautiful.

I spent so much time in his shop looking at these fascinating foods Tony nicknamed me 'Fish Face'. In later years I would serve Tony and his wife at Gabriel Machin's.

Tony opened a shop selling fish in Henley, along the Reading Road, opposite the Christ Church. During the day he sold wet fish and, in the evening, changed to hot fish and chips.

Living where we did in Wargrave, within beautiful countryside, we would often go out and forage for all the 'goodies' nature provided. Blackberries were a must for Mum's jam or crumble, and occasionally we might find some mushrooms. The fields on the Shiplake side of the river were often a good bet.

The river had an enormous influence on my life, as it had for many in the village. I learned to swim in the river. I had to, as I nearly drowned one day when I fell off a boat into the water. Someone saw what had happened and pulled me out, but Mum told me I couldn't go near the river again unless I learned to swim, so I did.

Summer holidays we filled, spending all our time by the river. A ferry took people across to the Shiplake side. I could get across and back for three pence! There was a sandy bay on the Shiplake side where we could swim. My sisters and I would take a drink and sandwiches, staying as long as we could.

Fishing became a favourite hobby, so I'd spend as much time as I could on the riverbank, either meeting up with friends or just on my own; I didn't mind as long as I could fish.

In later years when I'd started working, I managed to buy a small boat, allowing me to fish in places that had been out of reach, such as the Hennerton Backwater, or the River Loddon.

The biggest event of the year was the 'Wargrave and Shiplake Regatta', although I never took part in any of the boat races, I often watched them. The canoes, the skiffs, the gondola races in punts; they were all great. Another great fun activity was the Greasy Pole, watching people slide off, into the river.

There was also a funfair in the 60s, which I think was owned by the Traylen family, who travelled around the country to different venues. The fair was great fun, with its loud music, bumper car rides, and candy floss. I had my first shot with an air rifle there!

The village was full of people, all the pubs were overflowing day and night; there was a great atmosphere.

Around 10 pm the day's fun and festivities finished off with a fabulous firework display, which was always a brilliant end to an exciting day.

We found lovely chestnuts in the Autumn and my father would roast them over the fire. There were apple trees all around the village, and I must admit, I did sometimes raid the local orchard, scrumping! That was stealing, and something I wouldn't do now. Anyway, I am too old and slow!

I was expected to leave school at the age of fifteen and find a job, to bring money into the house, making things easier for Mum. It didn't take me long to establish where I wanted to be.

Chapter

2

Growing pains

On Monday 12th August 1968 I cycled from Wargrave to Henley, along with friends Bob Jones and Chris Hopes for the first day of our working lives. Bob was bound for the butchery department of the local Waitrose store and Chris was going to learn sign writing from his father, also called Chris, who was a well-respected local sign writer. Like Bob, I was going to learn butchery and headed for Gabriel Machin, Butchers in the Marketplace.

Sidney and Lilian Marett were the proprietors of Gabriel Machin at this time, working with their son Colin. Linda, my sister, was dating Colin, which is how I was offered the job. I was to work six days a week but would have Monday and Wednesday afternoons off, so five days' work. I would get three weeks' holiday and any bank holidays. I would be paid six pounds and ten shillings a week.

My initial motivation for working was to give Mum housekeeping money, helping her afford everything she needed for the family. My perception of what this huge change in my life meant was extremely limited. I'd never considered I wouldn't have enough time for important things like fishing, football, hanging out with mates, and talking about things like "Do you think the lady in the pub will sell us a bottle of cider if we tell her it's for Dad?"

Time had been going fast since starting work. I had hardly seen my mates, but I was enjoying learning about all the different cuts of meat and the routine in the shop, plus how and when we prepared everything.

Every Friday Sid went to 'Alf Meade' the abattoir in Reading. They would deliver eight lambs on a Monday morning. It became my job to cut the breasts and scrags (lamb necks) off all of them and remove the kidneys too. I often boned out the breasts and rolled them up with sage and onion stuffing inside, which made an inexpensive joint.

On Monday mornings we also made Cambridge Pork sausages and Beef sausages. It was my job to mix all the ingredients: meat, seasoning, dried rusk, and a little water, all minced together ready to be 'filled out' into skins and tied into strings of sausages.

The sausage-filling machine was an evil bit of kit! It had a barrel loaded with all the mix, with a nozzle on one end (which held the skin) and a plunger on the other end to push the meat out, into the skin. You would wind a handle to push the plunger up the barrel. You had to create quite a pressure behind the plunger to compact the sausages, and if your hand slipped off the handle it would fly back and give you a whack, which was painful. Also, if you hadn't loaded the barrel well enough, you may get air trapped, the result of which was an explosion of meat and skin flying everywhere!

Another responsibility I had was to make dripping. I'd chop up a large amount of beef suet, (fat alone wasn't good enough) then melt it all down and tip it into grease-proof paper containers. Dripping was very popular, as I think more people used that for cooking than they did oil.

The shop layout was quite different in 1968 to how it is in 2024. The big shop window bed had trays of meat displayed; mince, sausages, chops of pork and lamb, along with stewing meats, etc., and joints hung on rails above.

The small window area had a meat display too, but a different type. Here we displayed offal - hearts, livers, and kidneys; alongside pigs and sheep heads, all split in half, often sitting beside salted ox tongues and tripe. There were two cutting blocks, one on each side of the shop, and a small walk-in fridge at the back.

Molly Douglas, our cashier, sat in the small office next to the fridge. She would take payments from customers or take the details from those who had accounts with us. Molly did our wages every week.

The counter stood along the middle of the shop; on the top of which sat greaseproof paper and large sheets of brown paper, alongside weighing scales.

Thankfully, there were no plastic counter bags in those days, as our customers had bags or baskets. We did have plastic carrier bags, but people had to pay for those, which didn't always please them, as by this time the supermarkets had started to give them out for free, which I believe was the major contribution to the massive plastic problem the whole world has today.

A large part of my working day would be spent learning and being tutored by Colin.

Eddie Mann was one of our customers, he owned a Chinese Restaurant on Duke Street. One day Sid asked me to deliver an order to him, so I went to the restaurant and walked towards the kitchen when suddenly a waiter started shouting at me, pointing at the floor. Looking down I could see I had unwittingly left a trail of sawdust footprints all along the carpet, which he'd just vacuumed he informed me frantically. He was not a happy chap!

Sid would keep an eye on my work and bring to my attention anything he thought I could improve upon. I remember once I'd tied some beef joints and he fetched one out from the fridge, slapping it down on the block, whereupon all the strings came apart. Sid just said, "Not good enough, do it again; and you should check the others."

Sid would often catch me with an impractical joke. One day he asked me to go to the butcher around the corner in Duke Street and ask for the long weight. Well, the butcher kept me there for about 10 minutes and then explained that it was a joke amongst all the butchers, long wait, not long weight!

I wouldn't say Sid was a hard taskmaster, he simply let you know how important it was to be skilled at your job, as you had to work to the required standard, whatever you were doing. Sid had gained his skills in high-class businesses in London. He was a craftsman and enjoyed passing on his knowledge, particularly if you were keen, and showed some skill, along with an appetite for learning. He was intelligent and interesting. I enjoyed hearing his stories, particularly about his fishing exploits; he had some specimens he'd caught in the past displayed in glass cases.

As a fifteen or sixteen-year-old I wasn't exactly full of confidence, but acquiring the skills I did changed all that.

I always find watching a person displaying real skills they've learned a great pleasure, whether it be a baker, a musician, or any artist.

My cutting skills were improving very quickly, and I was often trusted to work untutored.

When the pigs arrived, they were whole carcasses, not split in half as they would be in later years. I learned how to carry one into the fridge and hang it up on my own. I was shown how to split them from the back legs down to the head, removing it, and leaving two sides.

We sold half or whole heads. Customers purchased pigs' heads to make into brawn; they're boiled, as are the trotters, which produce gelatine. All the meat was pulled off and made into brawn. The lambs' heads were also sold, as their brains were often floured and fried, and their tongues were boiled.

I cut the sides into joints and rolled the legs and shoulders (which were called spareribs in those days) into joints ready for selling. We would have three pigs every week. I was left to prepare them on my own. I was once approached by a customer, asking if I would go to his house and cut a side of pork that he'd bought from a friend who kept a few pigs; he'd set up a table in his garage for the purpose. I did that very occasionally in the evening after work, as I was always glad to earn a little extra money.

The shop would have at least two sides of beef every week. (meaning four quarters) I helped Colin prepare them, learning about the cuts and boning those that needed to be tied into joints, sirloins, briskets, and topside. The forerib was often sold as a boneless joint, but we cut a joint called 'wing rib' from the sirloin, which was sold with bones in it. The hind quarter had most of the prime cuts.

The forequarter's cuts had strange names; 'clod', which was used for stewing or mincing, and 'sticking', from the neck, was used for the same meals as 'clod'. I was told the name came from when the animal was slaughtered.

Another cut was 'Jacob's Ladder' which was a casserole 'slow cook' cut. I never did find out who Jacob was, but I assumed there was a biblical connotation. Colin showed me how to take the large bone from a leg of beef with five strokes of the knife! That was always a challenge!

Our chickens arrived eight to a box and came plucked, but still had their feet and heads, with their insides still intact too! We had to prepare them, making them oven ready. We'd always leave the giblets with them for purchase, as customers would use them to make stock for gravy, which gave it great flavour. A few of us would try and compete to see who could prepare them the fastest; having a box each, we would rush through them, however, we made sure they were prepared to our usual standards, ensuring they were very clean and ready to go on display in the shop.

The shop closed for lunch every day from one o'clock until a quarter past two, so we had a long break. During this time, I would often go exploring the town and its shops. There was so much more variety in Henley than in Wargrave.

There were two bakers; Lawlor's had two shops, one in the marketplace and one on Reading Road just past the Post Office, and Franco Belge had a double-fronted shop at the far end of Bell Street. I often bought lunch at Franco Belge, which was such an interesting shop: one side was all loaves of bread and rolls, and the other side was pies, pasties, beautiful cakes, donuts, eclairs, apple turnovers, and many more. While you were waiting for your turn to be served (as they were always busy) you could see the bakers working away, maybe taking bread from the oven. This added a wonderful aroma and warmth, adding to the atmosphere of what was a wonderful shop. I wish we had a baker just like that today.

Liptons was a grocery shop on Duke Street, selling bacon and ham, (amongst other things) which butchers didn't sell at that time. Sadly, for them, shopping habits were changing, and supermarkets sold all they did and more, the result of which was shop closures throughout the town, which was a real shame.

Frenches was another great shop on Duke Street; they were greengrocers, stocking a vast range of vegetables and fruits. Molly Heath worked there. Molly was a lovely lady who always made you feel she'd picked out the best produce in the shop for you. When Molly came into Machin's we always wanted to look after her well.

There were six other butchers' shops in town: Simmons and Sons on Reading Road, Appleton's on Duke Street, Gilbride on Hart Street, Dewhurst, Baxter's, and Druce and Craddock on Bell Street.

Besides these great shops, we had supermarkets; Tesco, Waitrose, and the Co-op, so plenty of choice if you were shopping for meat.

Hammants, although not a food shop, was so interesting you could buy anything from a shotgun to a motorbike, a TV, or a fridge freezer. I bought my first pop records there; you went into a booth to listen to them, deciding if you wanted to buy it. They also sold catapult elastic which as a young boy I found very handy!

Just around the corner from Machin's on Duke Street was Nuttalls, the sweet shop. I remember the very first time I went there. I was choosing what I was going to buy when suddenly from behind the counter a lady barked at me, "Put that back, that didn't go there!" I looked up to see this lady watching me; next to her was a smartly dressed man and I can remember thinking, 'Blimey mate, you have an old dragon there!'

Well, that old dragon I later found out was Blanche Nuttall and she was a lovely lady; a real pussy cat, not a dragon at all. Blanche taught me an important lesson, 'don't judge a person, try to understand them, and give everyone a chance, some are more complex than others. If after all that, they are still an arse, well at least you gave them the opportunity'.

I was enjoying the shop and the customers, and although initially I didn't serve, I was helping Lil to serve her customers, getting used to interacting with them, discovering their likes and dislikes.

I remember one day, I found myself behind the counter on my own and a lady came in, marched up to the counter, and said, "Have you any knackers, young man!" To say I was embarrassed is an understatement, I didn't know what to say. I thought 'Does she mean me personally or does she want some to eat?' I thought 'Do people really eat them?'

Anyway, I said, "No, sorry madam," and she went away. I found out later that sweetbreads are often thought by some people to be from that part of the anatomy, but they are in fact the pancreas gland on the lower end of the windpipe, before the lungs or the thymus gland in the throat.

Another customer I remember was a tall Scottish lady, Mrs. McDonald. She would stand in the queue, singing the Skye Boat song. If she asked for one pound of sausage, they had to be eights and one pound of mince had to be exact.

About six months after starting work, Jim Stansbury came to work with us, and being a similar age to me, we got on well. On our afternoons off we would go fishing or play snooker in the working men's club in Wargrave.

Jim had transport, a scooter, and if we were going to Wargrave, I (sitting on my bicycle) would hold onto Jim's arm and be towed along. In those days, (the late 1960's) there wasn't much traffic on the roads.

Although I enjoyed most aspects of work, at fifteen years of age I wasn't that prepared for the responsibilities that came my way and had no idea of the implications in store for me either. Work involved long hours, starting at 8:00 am and finishing at 5:30 pm. Early starts were six days a week.

I know I didn't always get to work on time. It was unfortunate some of my mates (who worked Monday to Friday) didn't work on Saturdays as I always did, so I didn't see them as much as before, so life felt quite different. I reckon it was two years before I fully appreciated and accepted what was required of me, as growing up was painful, and no doubt for my employer too.

Several events in those first two years at work shook me greatly. Firstly, I had a seizure at work which affected my confidence very badly. Epilepsy was to affect me for the next five years and disappeared as suddenly as it had started. Sidney became very ill and passed away, consequently, Colin had to take on the major responsibility of running the shop and I had to prove I was a very reliable backup, not just to Colin, but to Lilian too. Colin was very ambitious and hardworking, which would change Gabriel Machin's forever.

Chapter

3

Kcab Gnals

I expected to learn all about butchery, but I never realised I would learn a whole new language!

I'd excelled in French at school, but this 'butchers speak' was something quite different. Butchers back slang or 'Kcab Gnals' as they know it, is a way of talking amongst ourselves without involving others, particularly customers. We used it to inform each other about stock rotation. We might say use 'dlo eno', meaning use an old one; not necessarily old, but the first one to be used from all our fresh stock. But if a product was not in the best condition, we may say, 'Tib dlo mate'.

Occasionally a customer may come in and say, 'Morning rechtub', which would tell us they are (or have been) in the butchery trade.

With several young men working together, it wasn't unusual (after noticing an attractive customer) for one of us to say, 'Ecin namow ni the posh etam', and I, at seventeen would answer, 'Sey etam yrev ecin, doog gels but tib dlo rof me etam'.

Some market traders used the language, but I guess like most of these lovely traditions, they're now little used.

If you happen to walk into Machin's and say 'Morning rechtub' it may tell them you've read this book!

Chapter

4

Evolution

Colin and Linda married in 1971 and moved into a house on Elizabeth Road, Henley. Even more motivation to be successful at Gabriel Machin's shop.

The country in the 1970s was going through a tough time. Harold Wilson's Labour Party lost to the Conservatives under Ted Heath, but things were not going well, as some businesses were working a three- or four-day week, and there were frequent power cuts. There was a recession and high inflation. Some unions were striking for wage rises. Earnings weren't keeping up with inflation and more and more housewives were taking full-time employment, leaving less time for shopping, which influenced retailers and their marketing strategy.

It was decided we would offer bulk buys for the freezer. We were preparing 5lb packs of mince, chops, sausages, stewing beef, etc., all at a discount, and much more economical for our customers. Some customers bought half a pig, or a whole lamb, having it cut to their requirements.

We had several customers who persuaded friends to order with them, so instead of ordering one lamb, they may order three, bartering a better price.

So successful were these special offers that instead of our regular three pigs per week we often bought six, and instead of six or eight lambs we bought around twenty: a couple of times even thirty or forty! Luckily, we'd found a very good supplier of lamb, Edward Hamer who came from Llanidloes in mid-Wales.

The huge increase in turnover from the freezer trade put a strain on staff, who were expected to work extra hours to cope with all the preparation time needed to complete our orders, but the money earned in overtime did take some of the pain out of it.

Colin recognised the premises were inadequate for all the extra stock we needed to store, so embarked on restructuring the whole shop, particularly the areas to the rear.

The preparation room and fridge in the backyard were in poor condition, so it was demolished, and a new building was erected in its place, including a WC and sundries store, but no cold room. The walk-in cold room in the shop was removed, giving us room for another cutting block and a sink, which we hadn't had before, as the water for hand washing was brought into the shop with a bucket, always as full as possible from the boiler in the yard. At this time cross contamination was never an issue, even the environmental health inspectors didn't concern us, as we sold little else but fresh meats.

There was a large room behind the shop, which was the living room for the accommodation upstairs. It was decided this should be converted into a fridge, which gave us masses of storage.

Colin's brother, John, was a very good builder, so he was engaged to do most of the work.

The office had to be taken out to make way for the fridge, so John built a new office onto the side wall of the shop. This meant our cashier/bookkeeper Molly Douglas sat further into the retail area.

In those days we used chest freezers to 'freeze down' customer orders and store produce, but they were not up to the task, so Colin constructed a large 'walk-in' freezer in the backyard which we could use at Christmas time for turkey storage.

We had to store some birds in the old slaughterhouse, (now a garage) and prayed for cold weather to preserve them, as it wasn't refrigerated and left entirely to the elements. Once the birds were prepared for sale we could accommodate them in the fridge, however until then we couldn't, as we had little space suitable at that time.

The counter with weighing scales and wrapping paper was removed and replaced with a refrigerated display counter, and the front window display area was renewed and refrigerated, as previously it hadn't been.

All this refurbishment and new equipment came about over several years, paid for no doubt by the increase in footfall to the shop, but would prove to be a very wise investment.

Decimalisation was thrust upon us early in 1971. The new 5, 10, and 50 pence pieces replaced the older familiar Tanners, Bobs, and Half-Crowns. This 'new money' just didn't have that same familiar feeling about it. When Molly gave me my weekly wages, £7.50 sounded as though I'd had money deducted.

Simmons and Sons closed in the early 1970s, followed by Dewhurst and Druce & Craddock, later the same decade.

Fred Hancock, who was the butchery manager at the Co-op, retired and came to work for us, making our sausages every Tuesday and Friday. Freddie was full of stories about Henley in the past and remembered the slaughterhouse at the back of the shop being used and the animals being herded from the market, which was by the railway station along Reading Road, or sometimes up Friday Street to Greys Road, then up Tuns Lane to the slaughterhouse.

Freddie was a very proud Englishman and had many other stories about wartime. He'd initially joined us on a part-time basis at Machin's when we were short-staffed but stayed for 14 years before retiring completely.

Staffing was always a problem; many people came and worked for two or three years and then left to try something else. I know the long hours were a major issue for most staff, as some stated they could work shorter hours for more money in other trades, but the thing I found very disappointing was that most said they enjoyed their time working in the shop.

The shop was going from strength to strength with customer numbers expanding all the time, with our range of produce being added to regularly.

Our beef was always purchased from the abattoir in Reading and occasionally from another wholesaler, but we wanted more quality and consistency, so Colin started going to Smithfield market in London, which gave us access to products we hadn't sold before. We could now stock veal every week. The escallops and chops were very popular. We also stocked 'Osso Buco' which I had never heard of before. Calves' liver was also a big seller.

The veal was originally reared in Holland. Some customers had issues concerning the way the calves were kept in barns or reared in crates to stop them from getting out and eating the grass, as that would affect the colour of the meat. The European market called for very pale meat, consequently, their diet was often milk-based to ensure white meat. Many male calves from dairy herds in England were sold to Holland to be raised for veal.

We felt it was important at Machin's to learn the provenance and farming practices of our suppliers. English Rose veal wasn't even mentioned at this time. There probably wasn't sufficient interest to market it.

We got our Guinea fowl, duck breasts, (and legs), quail, poussin, and smoked chickens from France regularly. Although we had always stocked game, we were now going into it in a big way. Pheasants and Partridge were purchased from local estates, many from the Bix shoot, owned by Lord Alvingham and usually delivered by Fred Phillpot, their gamekeeper. We also got a few from the Hambleden shoot where I believe George Brown was the keeper.

One season we guaranteed to buy all the pheasant the Hambleden shoot could supply, amounting to probably 7,000 birds. We had to pluck and prepare them all and offered customers three brace (6 birds) for £12.00. They were so popular we could hardly prepare them quickly enough. I would often pluck four birds in my lunch break, earning a little more money. A few local people came to pluck pheasants for us too, but we got a plucking machine eventually, which made the job much quicker. Mum plucked pheasants at home for us too! My sister Linda delivered them to her, picking them up plucked and ready two days later. Mum was very slow at plucking, but extremely meticulous, never splitting the skin. You could always tell which she'd plucked, they were immaculate.

Late in the 1970s, Colin introduced produce termed 'charcuterie', a new name to me. This included salami, liver sausage, pate, French speciality sausages, Toulouse, Boudin Blanc, and occasionally Andouillete and Parma ham; all of which came from a specialist supplier in London called Robinski.

All these fabulous new foods were proving to be extremely popular, with our food knowledge growing all the time.

Our first cheeses were introduced during the Christmas period in the late 1970s. We started with Stilton and Montgomery Cheddar. The customers were very enthusiastic about them. Colin was confident we would soon have an extensive range.

I have to say I have been fascinated with cheese since my earliest recollections, starting with my wandering around the International Stores in Wargrave.

Colin wanted to sell hams at Christmas, so for a few years we bought gammons from the Danish bacon company in Reading and cooked many of them ourselves. They were so popular we always sold out.

We purchased some superb foods, like gammons, which our customers thoroughly enjoyed. However, Colin realised we could produce these ourselves, and of the same, if not better quality, but at less cost to us.

Sid and Lilian had an appreciation of top-quality food, which Colin had inherited. The success of the business was built on those principles.

Chapter

5

Wonderful fromage

As previously mentioned, I was fascinated by cheese from a very young age; its size, shape, smell, and how it was cut, everything about it.

Gabriel Machin stocked Colston Bassett Stilton and Montgomery cheddar for Christmas, which I'd never heard of before working there, but I was to learn that these were the superior varieties of British cheese.

A shop had opened along Reading Road by the stonemasons called Wells Stores, (later the Granary) who sold cheeses the like of which I had never seen before: Cotherstone, Castle Cary Cheddar, Brie de Meaux, and many others. I often found myself drawn to that shop during my lunch break. I would occasionally buy a small piece, but I thought they were very expensive, so I often just window-shopped!

Sometime later I watched a TV program about a local man, Patrick Rance, whose father owned two of the Wells Stores' cheese shops; one in Streatley and the one I visited in Henley-on-Thames. He talked about showing cheeses. He had written a book called 'The Great British Cheese Book', so I just had to buy one! I would urge all cheese lovers to buy a copy. I know it was researched in the 1970s and written in 1982, so the list of cheeses is nothing as exhaustive as it would list today, but the history and facts are worth it alone, which will always be of interest.

Patrick Rance is without doubt the godfather of British farmhouse cheese, mainly for the way he encouraged and stood up for the traditional farmhouse cheesemakers during very difficult times, particularly after the Second World War. After I'd read his book, I felt the cork had been taken out of the bottle and I was drinking it all in, and I still am.

Colin (after our success with Christmas cheese) wanted to stock a variety regularly, so he purchased a refrigerated display cabinet and asked me to purchase 10 new cheeses to sell alongside the two we already had. I'd seen a van from a London cheese wholesaler locally, so I phoned them, asking to recommend some varieties we might stock.

Two days later our new cheeses arrived. From day one our cheeses sold fantastically well, consequently, we needed deliveries every week. Our customers were asking for new cheeses, so I added them to our selection regularly. I was in my element, as sampling cheese was new to me, as was gaining the knowledge of all the makers of milk, types of cow, sheep, or goat, and whether they were pasteurised or unpasteurised - 'au lait cru' as the French term it.

We came to understand that most cheeses made with unpasteurised milk had a greater depth and a more complex flavour.

Montgomery cheddar at its best has the most amazing complex flavour you could ever wish for and is always made with unpasteurised milk from the farm. I have never found a pasteurised cheddar that comes anywhere near it for flavour.

The cheese fridge at Machin's

Most makers of block cheddar use milk from several farms which may vary in quality, and pasteurisation neutralises any difference in quality, thereby producing a bog-standard product.

Colston Bassett Stilton was originally made with unpasteurised milk, but that practice was dropped many years ago and I believe theirs is the finest Stilton made today. For many people, Stilton is a Christmas cheese, but I think it's great anytime.

Scott[*] on his first expedition to the Antarctic took twelve whole Stilton rounds with him and came back safe and sound. Sadly, on his second expedition, he didn't take any Stilton and didn't make it back, so you should eat Stilton anytime! It's obviously good for you!

---

[*]Robert Falcon Scott CVO (6 June 1868 – c. 29 March 1912) was a British Royal Navy officer and explorer who led two expeditions to the Antarctic regions: the *Discovery* expedition of 1901–04 and the *Terra Nova* expedition of 1910–13.

As much as I liked to stock and sell cheeses all year round, I would have to concede there were some cheeses I would consider as seasonal; Burrata and Mozzarella are cheeses I particularly enjoy with summer fruits, especially peaches and green salad leaves, alongside Iberica ham. Raclette is considered a winter cheese, particularly popular during the skiing season, and often served partially melted and great with salami, cured meats, small potatoes, and cornichons. Another dish synonymous with the skiing season is Tartiflette, which is made with Reblochon cheese. I consider this more of a winter cheese.

Colin recognised my enthusiasm and growing knowledge of many varieties of cheese. I loved my work, and the fact I was lucky to be afforded the freedom to do so, receiving so much encouragement to expand our range.

My knowledge of producers and suppliers grew and grew. Neal's Yard Dairy was one producer who matured their cheeses, and rave reviews were heard everywhere, so we decided to get some of their cheese in to sell. We were delighted we made this decision, as they were of fantastic quality, and a step up from most other suppliers, however, they only supported producers of British cheese, which meant we had to source Comte and Roquefort elsewhere.

We even sold apples! Those in season were also purchased through Neal's Yard. They came from the Brogborough Horticultural Trust in Kent. This started another fascination for me, apples and pears!

Randolph Hodgson, the owner of Neal's Yard Dairy, took on the mantle Patrick Rance had started with his support for makers of traditional farmhouse British cheeses; many others joined him, including James Aldridge who made cheese and taught many others. They started in the late 1970s - a real renaissance of British cheese making that had been under threat of extinction, save for a few enthusiasts since the post-war years.

We couldn't have started our cheese counter in Machin's at a more fortuitous time. Gaining knowledge of British cheeses was a voyage of discovery; where it's made, who makes it, and the type of milk used. We were in the middle of a great wave of enthusiasm for new cheese appearing on our shelves.

Waterloo Cheese was made under the 'Village Maid' banner, produced by Ann Wigmore in Spencer's Wood, on the outskirts of Reading. This cheese originally contained milk from Guernsey cows farmed on the Duke of Wellington's estate near Reading. She also made a soft sheep's milk cheese called 'Wigmore' and a hard sheep's milk cheese called 'Spenwood'. These sat alongside other British cheeses; Kirkham's Lancashire, and Appleby's Cheshire, which contains annatto, a flavourless vegetable dye, making it a lovely orange colour.

We also stocked Elmhirst and Ticklemore cheeses from Devon and Stinking Bishop made by Charles Martel from Gloucestershire, which has a bark stronger than its bite!

We soon got into French cheeses, and the range was huge. Some were well-known, such as Brie and Roquefort for example, which were soon joined by St Nectarie, Beaufort, Morbier, Epoisse, and Tomme Da Savoie. I discovered there are dozens of Tomme cheeses.

France is very proud of its cheese and has a government body, the AOC (Appellation D'origier Controlee) which sets out regulations the cheesemakers must follow to gain accreditation for their cheese. There are twenty-two regions in France and very often a cheese must be made in a specific one and in a specific manner to be allowed to carry that name. Comte is a cheese I immediately fell in love with and in time found that those bearing the name of Marcel Petite were consistently wonderful. They are made near a village called St Antoine in the Jura mountains and aged in an old military Fort built into the mountain which maintains a perfect, cool, and damp atmosphere. Vacherin Mont D'or is another interesting cheese and only available from October to March. The milk must come from cows that graze in the mountains at 700 metres or higher. The attention to detail that fromages in France learned to exercise over countless years has now been replicated by many who make or mature cheeses in Britain.

We also stocked an Irish cheese called Cashel Blue. A relative of the Grubb family from County Tipperary would buy some for Christmas if he wasn't likely to be in Ireland for the season.

I once conversed with Graham Kirkham about his fabulous Lancashire cheese; he now matures them at 10 degrees, finding that encourages a much deeper flavour.

Neals Yard matures many of its cheeses in rooms underground, replicating the method of the French with theirs, regarding temperature and humidity. The maturation of cheese I found very interesting. Hard cheeses (cheddar etc.) seemed obvious, but as my knowledge grew, I began to understand a little about the techniques employed in their making, the application of temperature to the milk, the microflora contained in the milk, which together with bacteria contributes to the flavours found in the cheese.

You also have washed rind cheeses, some that are termed 'mould-ripened', and the softer cheeses; the maturation of which I found a little difficult to understand.

One observation I had was that mould-ripened cheeses often have wrinkly rinds when aged, much like people!

I was on a voyage of discovery; tasting new cheeses that were simply amazing. I instantly wanted to share that pleasure, wanting to bring that enjoyment to everyone, and I wanted to experience that pleasure with appreciative like-minded people, and still do!

Christmas 2001 Colin presented me with a book called 'The Cheese Room' written by Patricia Michelson, who, like me, has a love affair with cheese. The book was inscribed with the words '2001, a memorable year for cheese'.

We achieved record sales and supplied a greater selection than ever. The recipes in Patricia's book are rather special, in particular the sublime pesto and cheeseburger.

Some farmers turn to cheese making when their milk gives a poor financial return. Rose Grimond of Nettlebed Creamery had that problem, and now thankfully achieves wonderful results by producing 3 pasteurised cow's milk cheeses, all superior quality from her beautiful Montbeliard cattle.

British cheesemaking has come a long way in the past 30 years and the cheese counter in Gabriel Machin enabled us to learn another trade, another string to the bow, plus made the business more attractive and viable financially.

I salute Rose Grimond and Anne Wigmore for the results achieved with their cheeses, and especially Patrick Rance, who I consider the catalyst for the health of British cheesemaking today.

Strange but true, I can remember all these years later the first time I tasted Montgomery Cheddar, but I can't remember the first pint of beer I had. The cheese had a wonderful flavour and lingered in my memory, but perhaps I didn't stop at one pint!

Chapter 6

Fishes La Mer

Colin and I have a conundrum, like the chicken and egg, 'What came first at Gabriel Machin's? Fish or cheese?' Neither of us can remember, suffice to say we know they were both introduced around 1980.

Colebrookes had a fish stall in Duke Street, Henley, which I think closed in the very early 1970's.

Tony Shaw had a fish shop briefly on Reading Road, and later in the 70s MacFisheries had a shop on Bell Street, however, it closed after a decade or so.

Colin was shopping in town one day when a lady stopped him, saying, "I wish you sold fish too!". Well, that got him thinking. He was regularly travelling to Smithfield Market in London, so on his next trip he decided to divert to the Billingsgate Fish Market and buy a small selection, just to see if customers were interested in buying them. Lilian didn't think that selling fish was a good idea, as she'd tried it sometime beforehand, and sadly, it hadn't been a success.

The following day our fish display (containing plaice, cod, salmon, smoked haddock, and lemon soles) was arranged, and beautifully laid out in our refrigerated counter.

The ice we'd made in our freezer, which we'd constructed in the backyard. We used to 'mince' the ice, which started as large blocks from our industrial-sized machine.

Thankfully, the fish was well received by our customers. It's fair to say one or two people were not keen on us handling fish as well as their meat purchases, but overall, it appeared a promising move. We were soon getting regular requests from customers for species we were not stocking, so our selection, like our cheese, was growing all the time.

No member of staff had any real experience in fish preparation, so we were all learning on the job, but because we had knife skills, most techniques were gained quickly.

Lobsters and crabs usually arrived to us live, so we cooked those in our big boiler in the yard.

We had several requests for whole cooked salmon but had no way to cook one until a chef suggested we put one in the sink and cover it with boiling water for half an hour, which we did, only to find the fish wasn't cooked through. We knew a fish kettle was used for cooking salmon, but those commonly available were not large enough for the fish we had.

One of our customers, John Hill, made various metal utility items, so he made us several kettles of different sizes, enabling us to cope with any cooking we needed to do. We discovered the kettles were better than the boiler for crabs and lobsters. Over the years those kettles saw a lot of service, particularly during Henley Regatta, when we would cook and dress maybe 30 salmon.

Marlin Monroe

Squid Vicious

Prawn Connery

Anchovy Hopkins

Dressing the fish was a superb finishing touch; laying thin cucumber slices all over the body, arranged so they resembled scales; the eye would be removed, and a stuffed olive put in its place, then sliced lemon would be placed all around the salver, tucked under the edge of the fish, then finally some prawns added, finishing the decoration. The dressing procedure is still the same today, more than 30 years later.

The salvers were too big to fit in a standard fridge, so if a customer wanted a fish for an occasion, I'd meet them at the shop on a Sunday morning. I'd tell them to put some ice in a large container (even a bath!) and position the salver on top, then the fish would be fine.

We did lose a few salvers over time, but that was our fault for not keeping records and reminding people to return them.

Smoked salmon was a particular favourite of Colin's, so he occasionally bought some when he was in Billingsgate. He became very interested in finding out how to smoke some for himself, so he read all he could about the processes involved.

There was no smokehouse at Machin's, so Colin had to make one for himself and went looking for something big enough to hold a side of salmon, and most importantly, have enough room for a firebox.

He found the right article, a wardrobe! So, Machin's first smoked salmon was produced in a wardrobe!

Colin's growing confidence steered him to build a smokehouse, ideally located where the old slaughterhouse sat, i.e. the old garage at the back of the premises. The smokehouse was built into the back corner of the room. Colin was confident it would work, as the chamber went from the ground floor to the ceiling of the first floor, which meant we could probably accommodate up to 100 sides of salmon, all hanging on cut-down broom handles, perched on posts screwed into the wall, usually eight sides per pole.

A firebox was loaded with cut-down logs of oak and had a lid that could be positioned across the top, so you could control the amount of smoke. A fan was positioned within the roof, which would draw the smoke over the salmon and out of the chamber. This would then dissipate into the atmosphere.

If there was low cloud cover and little wind, the smoke would hang low. One day the local fire engine came racing up Tuns Lane, as a member of the public had reported the building was on fire!

Gabriel Machin's smoked salmon became phenomenally successful in a very short time. When we originally processed it, we were buying fish from Billingsgate Fish Market, but soon found another supplier who (because of the volume we were buying) gave us a better price.

HOLY SMOKE! A BUTCHER SELLING FISH

We also considered his fish (coming from a smaller farm) of superior quality.

Most of the fish we smoked were from farmed stock, but a smaller amount was wild fish (when in season) and a wild fish in beautiful condition produced the most amazing smoked salmon you could ever imagine.

We occasionally smoked wild sea trout, which was also wonderful.

We were recommended by (and listed by) the Scottish Quality Salmon Board as a supplier of superior-quality salmon. When the fish arrived from the supplier they had a tag on their gills, advertising their superior quality.

In the early days of selling fish, wild salmon and sea trout were plentiful in season and Colin would sometimes go to Billingsgate on a Saturday, as the traders might have some bargains. They would be closed until Tuesday, and not want to be left with stock.

It wasn't unusual for Colin to return with two large boxes of grilse (small young wild salmon) and two boxes of wild sea trout, which we would offer to customers at a very reasonable price, endeavouring to sell all that day, which we invariably did.

On one occasion, Colin arrived back from the market with a small box and said, "Look at these little beauties, they're smoked sprats!" We all sampled them there and then; they were gorgeous!

We sold them regularly from then on, as customers appreciated how good they were. The smoked salmon garnered a wonderful following.

One of our regular customers worked for British Airways. The Catering Manager for BA was so impressed with our salmon he decided he wanted to serve it on Concorde flights. Praise indeed!

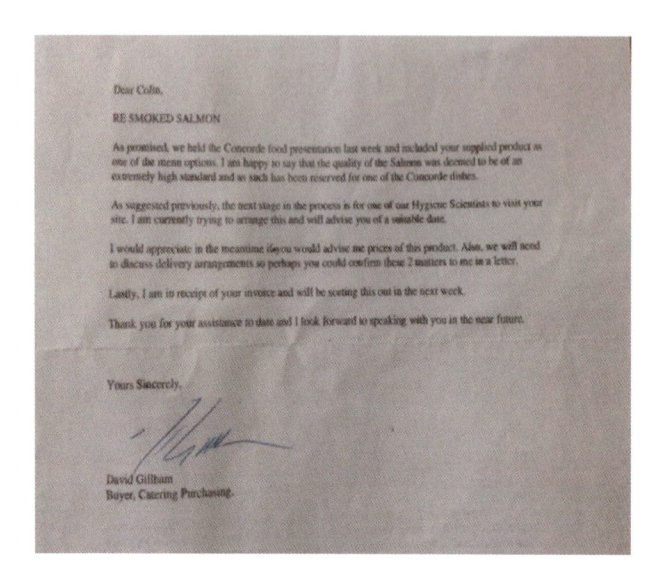

> Dear Colin,
>
> RE SMOKED SALMON
>
> As promised, we held the Concorde food presentation last week and included your supplied product as one of the menu options. I am happy to say that the quality of the Salmon was deemed to be of an extremely high standard and as such has been reserved for one of the Concorde dishes.
>
> As suggested previously, the next stage in the process is for one of our Hygiene Scientists to visit your site. I am currently trying to arrange this and will advise you of a suitable date.
>
> I would appreciate in the meantime if you would advise me prices of this product. Also, we will need to discuss delivery arrangements so perhaps you could confirm these 2 matters to me in a letter.
>
> Lastly, I am in receipt of your invoice and will be sorting this out in the next week.
>
> Thank you for your assistance to date and I look forward to speaking with you in the near future.
>
> Yours Sincerely,
>
> David Gillham
> Buyer, Catering Purchasing.

We found a great packaging supplier who helped us design some for our half-pound packs and sides of salmon. The design had a fisherman logo on it and was ahead of its time in terms of quality.

We had many customers who fished for salmon and trout, bringing their catch to us for smoking.

One customer (a famous sports commentator) left four salmon with us to smoke. I was left to deal with them. Sadly, I made the mistake of leaving the lid off the firebox, the result of which was well-cooked, not smoked salmon! We had to buy replacement fish from the market, and I think they were better quality than the fish he left with us! Fishermen were of course proud of their catch, but they weren't always of the best quality.

Having our own smoking house had a huge impact on the business. We started smoking eels and Rick Stein (the well-known chef) wrote a book praising food producers in Britain and we were included for our smoked produce, which was a feather in our cap!

Me, with Richard Mackie

Article in the Henley Standard – 'All smiles for salmon – Terry Colby and Richard Mackey show off two of Machin's finest fish to celebrate the shop's appointment as Henley's official salmon retailer.'

The confidence gained as a business from our smoking venture encouraged Colin to buy a smoker for our meat products, which I mention in another chapter.

Mum didn't cook fish very often when we were growing up. It was probably too expensive for a large family, but I do remember Dad buying some cod from Tony Shaw and when he unwrapped it at home we noticed some tiny worms on it, so he returned it to the shop and Tony explained that parasites occasionally affected fish, and changed it for a new one. Many fish attract parasites; cod, mackerel, and hake seemed to be the worst affected.

I'd only ever cooked cod, and occasionally smoked haddock myself until we started selling fish at Machin's. However, this fabulous selection motivated me to try many others! Lemon sole became a favourite, also sprats, smoked mackerel, hake, halibut, and monkfish all followed, as I became more confident with cooking.

A lady called Carmen, who was a housekeeper and cook at a local house, came every week and bought fish from us. We often talked together about her favorite fish, and one day she kindly cooked a paella for me, which was lovely, and I thoroughly enjoyed it, except for the mussels! I struggled with their texture, which I found alien.

Something I came to love, which has a very soft texture, is herring roe, fried to a slight crisp on the edges, on toast made from proper baker's bread, with a squeeze of lemon and black pepper – absolute heaven!

My three children, Joanna, Alex, and Rebecca grew up with no phobias, hang-ups, or fears about food. I used to take many things home that they could help to prepare, or at least sample foods they weren't used to eating. I took home some sprats which they helped to clean, taking their heads off, etc. We would flour and fry them, then eat them with bread and butter. Kippers too, with all their bones. Pig's liver casserole was another meal, and they all seemed to enjoy it.

I saw a recipe for fish pie, not the sort that has mashed potato, (although I do like that too!) but had smoked haddock, cod, and a small quantity of salmon, all lightly poached then flaked together, topped with sliced boiled eggs and a cheesy sauce; all wrapped up in a puff pastry case; all three kids loved it! I enjoyed cooking that pie in early summer when local asparagus was available to accompany it.

Our success with the fish counter showed what you could achieve with diversification, something other food shops in town didn't do, (or were unable to) which may have led to their demise. Supermarkets were proving very attractive, so we had to protect our position as much as we could, which we were doing very successfully.

Colin travelled to two markets in London every Tuesday and Friday, which meant getting up at 3 am, visiting both markets and returning to the shop, then working the rest of the day. This was understandably taking its toll.

A local chap, Jose Vital, visited both markets and supplied nearby restaurants and pubs. Colin did a deal with him – Jose would pick up our meat order from Smithfield and buy all the fish we needed. During this time fewer fishmongers used the Billingsgate market. They were buying directly from brokers instead.

We started trading with 'La Mer', a company that bought all species of fish from fishermen and markets all around Britain and sold over the phone to shops like ours, (and caterers) having them delivered to you by refrigerated transport the next day. We soon built up a good relationship with La Mer and spoke to the same salesperson every day. They soon understood we were always requiring the best quality fish, often coming from day boat fishermen, rather than trawlers, where the fish can be several days old before being offered for sale.

Within a few short years, our fish counter contained a diverse selection, with some customers coming in to solely buy fish and no meat at all, as some customers did with our cheese. We took that as a compliment, as the quality spoke for itself, vindicating Colin's decision to diversify the business as he did.

One product we bought from Billingsgate transported me back to Tony Shaw's shop in Wargrave – gulls' eggs. We had several customers who bought them every week, although the season was very short. Transporting them was always a challenge, because they were expensive, and you couldn't afford to break any. Jose Vital was never happy when he had to deliver those to us!

On investigating my family history (with the help of my grandson Finn) I discovered one of my ancestors (in the 18th century) was a very respected fish merchant in Lowestoft, Suffolk! Was I always destined to be in the food trade and sell fish?

Chapter

7

Christmas

When I first joined Machin's, it was well supported and has been ever since, with regular Friday and Saturday queues, however, Christmas queues were another level! The volume of customer orders increased dramatically from early November. Molly would take their details and record them all alphabetically in her journal.

Footfall would increase every week, reaching an upsurge on the 22nd, through to Christmas Eve, when all the collections took place.

It was challenging work during the Christmas period in the early days, however that was nothing compared with what was to come in later years.

The first Christmas I was at Machin's, Sid created a display that was placed in the window overnight, advertising our Christmas stock to everyone walking by. I thought it looked fantastic; big trays of meats and sides of pork hanging at the back with turkeys, chickens, and lambs.

We cleaned our windows with a product called 'whitening' which was fine ground chalk; this, with a little water added made a slightly abrasive cleaner and could also be used as a medium for writing on the glass.

Sid used this to paint robins and snowflakes on the window for Christmas, creating a highly effective Christmassy feeling. In later years Colin and I created larger ones, with turkeys, geese, capons, ribs, and sides of beef, with sides of pork hanging behind; if the weather were cold, we could leave a quarter of beef hanging in the shop for a few days.

I remember one Christmas a customer gave us a bottle of champagne, which we drank steadily through the day. Consequently, lifting a quarter of beef into the shop was a very giggly affair, as we laughed so much, we couldn't lift it! Sadly, some years we were so busy we didn't have the time to design a display. We purchased prize-winning sides of beef at Christmas, making them the centrepiece in our displays.

We purchased all the turkeys we needed (and we needed many!) from Donald Dawes, who farmed at Park Place farm on Remenham Hill. Don only reared turkeys for the Christmas market and employed local people temporarily to help with the plucking and prep. In later years we bought turkeys from Tom Copas, before finding Pat Lambert, located near Thame, who is the supplier the shop still uses today in 2024.

John Homewood from Peach Croft farm near Abingdon produced top-quality geese, so we always made sure we got sufficient in stock for the season. John's son Bill took over the farm and with his wife Kim continued the good work, and thankfully Gabriel Machin is still a customer of his today. Bill Homewood is recognised in the trade as one of the finest poultry producers in the country and happens to be one of the nicest, most genuine fellas you are ever likely to meet.

Poultry in years gone by never arrived oven ready. We had to prepare every one of them, and when you consider we sold 400 or more turkeys, 50 plus geese, and dozens of ducks and capons, you can appreciate how much work it created for us. We had a team of four or five people for at least three days to prepare all the poultry.

Linda had three boys, (Christopher, Daniel, and Nicholas) who all helped at Christmas; primarily Chris who was slightly older. He came with one or two of his school friends to lend a hand. Chris could also make sausages, which was a bonus. Colin's brother John usually took one or two weeks away from his building business to help too.

Quite a few turkeys were hung outside the shop front on rails under the canopy. Customers would pick a turkey out to their required size, then we would label it with their name, and arrange for them to pick it up later.

In those early days, there was no blind on the shop front, so we could regularly hang game and rabbits out there. One day we opened after lunch and found we had lost a brace of pheasants!

When I was growing up, I noticed butchers didn't usually sell gammon and ham, as these products were typically sold by grocers. However, Colin decided to branch out and offer these items too. He purchased 50 smoked gammons from the Danish Bacon company in Reading. Some of the gammons were cooked and sold, while others were sold raw for people to cook at home. We sold all 50 in no time at all, so the following year we ordered 80, many of which were hung in the shop. I thought the aroma was amazing, as did the customers.

As far back as I can remember, the aromas in food shops have given me immense pleasure, whether it's a real baker baking his bread, ground coffee beans, a deli, (where they may have continental hams hanging in the shop) a fishmonger, or butcher shop. All these are missing in supermarkets, where most of the produce is sterile, wrapped in plastic, and often served to you by staff with no in-depth knowledge of what they are selling, and sadly, with little enthusiasm.

Richard Mackie, Colin Marett, and me

I accept that supermarkets are now part of our way of shopping but feel that we have been seduced into giving away a quality that was once ours.

We stocked DBC gammon for years until Colin heard of a pig farmer in Wiltshire who cured his bacon and gammon, which proved to be of excellent quality, so we bought from him. Within a few short years, we were buying two hundred gammons from him at Christmas, and we cooked over one hundred, glazing them with syrup and demerara sugar, then studding them with cloves. Machin's Christmas ham became a favourite in Henley and further afield.

Linda would come and work in the shop at Christmas, being responsible for ham glazing and very conscientious about their care and appearance. Linda also made extremely popular game pies, and we always sold out.

Henley town organised a Christmas festival for late-night shopping which (if memory serves) took place on the first Friday in December and ran till 9:00 PM.

Colin decided we would have a BBQ outside the shop, serving jumbo sausages and bacon rolls. Anthony Worrall Thompson came to help cook and serve, which he continued to do for years. Sometimes his wife Jay joined as well.

The barbeque always attracted hundreds of customers, thrilled to be attended by a famous chef.

We also served tasters of cheese and smoked salmon in the shop, recommending various exclusive offers. I remember on one occasion we sold around 40 packs of smoked salmon. Late-night shopping proved to be an effective way to advertise the business, while at the same time earning money for doing so.

The smokehouse was usually full of salmon, smoked through the evening. We took groups of people to view the impressive site, but Colin had to stop sadly, as we had a burglary. We thought someone with criminal intent, on viewing the smokehouse, viewed the layout of the premises at the same time.

The 23rd and the 24th of December were always the manic trading days, with new products stocked year on year. The Christmas queue of customers grew and grew. Consequently, word spread, and we became famous for our food. Having to provide so much stock in a short space of time, it became impossible not to have a queue. Customers would often enquire as to when they should pick up their order, "When would be a quiet time?" The answer was frequently, "January Madam."

Linda used to make hundreds of mince pies, handing them to the queuing customers, along with mulled wine. The Christmas queue at Machin's, with its festive fair, became a tradition for us all, including our customers, which they would not miss.

Our successful smoked salmon was essential for many customers at Christmas; however, time management was a real issue.

Colin didn't like to 'freeze and store' any of our produce in advance of the Christmas rush, as he was very proud of our smoking capabilities and felt freezing anything would take away from that, so he tried to prepare everything as close to Christmas as possible, supplying fresh to our customers, so they could then freeze the foods if they wished at home themselves.

One year, between October and December, we smoked around 1000 sides. It was not unusual to start work at 5:30 am and then struggle to finish by midnight. Often a week's work at Christmas amounted to about one hundred hours, working every day, from the 1st to the 24th. Colin always paid us well with overtime and was not shy in showing his appreciation for our efforts. On Christmas Eve our customers were very generous too.

One of our customers (who worked for an airline) used to sell us top-quality Russian caviar. I remember one Christmas we sold 50g tins for twenty-five pounds each, which added £2000 to our takings.

The shop was demanding at Christmas, the long working hours, and the pace you had to work at, however, I loved it, and found it exciting, whilst being carried along on an adrenaline wave.

The stock levels were huge for a couple of weeks, extending into the new year, which was also a busy time.

When buying cheeses, I didn't have to be cautious, and ambition took over! I was safe in the knowledge that we were likely to sell them all.

Colston Bassett Stilton produced a 'baby' edition, aimed at the Christmas trade. We usually sold around thirty, but one year we had so many orders we sold fifty-five of them alone.

I used this ideal time of increased footfall to introduce samples of new cheeses, offering samples to the queueing customers, and gauging their reactions; this helped me too, as it was a great opportunity to gain experience together, becoming acquainted with a new cheese we could later stock if it proved popular enough.

Pate de Foie Gras, (for some a controversial item because of the traditional means of production) became a staple stock item, being extremely popular. We bought 500g blocks and cut them according to customer requirements.

Colin had holidayed in France one summer and found a supplier of duck confit, goose fat, and Cassoulet. The following Christmas we bought direct from them, a whole pallet load! The shop became jam-packed with tins! We sold an amazing amount, even supplying other butchers with them, particularly goose fat which wasn't readily available at that time.

I enjoyed the Cassoulet, and it was only a matter of time before I acquired a recipe and made it at home. Yes, it takes time, the best of two days, but it was so worth it: a wonderful autumn /winter dish.

We recognised the superior quality of products from France. Colin made numerous trips to the Rungis Market in Paris, returning with foie gras and smoked chicken. Buying these items was the main motive for going, however, he also gained great knowledge of the meat cuts available there, which we could adopt in the shop.

Chapter

8

Personalities

We were attracting a larger customer base, due to the diversity and quality of the range we offered. Amongst these new customers were TV presenters, actors, musicians, writers and artists of various kinds; people whom some call celebrities.

Many people who are well known because of their vocation are very happy to go about their business, shopping etc., with no recognition, just like the rest of us, but I always enjoyed meeting them, to see what their personality was really like, in daily life, opposed to how they may come across on TV, etc.

Dave Allen, the comedian, was a regular customer. He was great fun when he came into the shop, and as funny as he was on TV. When we weighed his steak, he wanted to put his 'half finger' on the scales. He said this was because it would be cheaper than us putting our thumb on it. We half expected him to pull up a stall and sit there, telling us funny stories, all while having a drink or smoking a cigarette, as he did regularly in his show.

Jean Marsh, the actress, was a lady with an attractive sense of humour. At Christmas when ordering a turkey, she insisted that it needed to be perfectly formed, free range, all singing all dancing, and a young bird - no more no less. She also showed much empathy when a personal tragedy struck us; she was a very sincere lady.

I was a young man in the 1970s, and very much into my music, so when John Lord and Ian Paice of the rock band Deep Purple became customers, I thought that was great.

Ian Piace came into the shop once carrying an LP, so I asked him what it was. He showed me the LP, recorded by a group called the 'Pink Fairies'. I have to say when listening to it later, I wasn't impressed with their name or their music! I was to find out later what a talented musician John Lord was, and his talent wasn't confined to the rock genre.

Having recognisable people shopping with us became an almost daily occurrence; so starstruck we were not, but I did on one occasion have to serve Rod Stewart. You could feel the atmosphere in the shop, particularly among the lady customers, who were all aware of who he was. He came in to order a turkey for Christmas. I felt silly having to ask him his name, so I asked his girlfriend who was a young blonde lady, who I think was Swedish.

They were staying locally for Christmas, but I never saw who collected their order.

Robert Hardy 'star of stage and screen' had an account at Machin's and would often send a cheque, accompanied by a very eloquently written note, stating how much he'd enjoyed his purchases.

Björn Ulvaeus from ABBA and his wife Lena Källersjö lived near Henley for a time and shopped in Machin's. I remember they gave Colin a recipe for Gravadlax, which I know Colin still has.

Simon Williams, the well-known actor, came in regularly, as did his wife Lucy Fleming.

Raymond Blanc's mother-in-law was a customer too. Raymond was researching recipes for a book he was writing, so we acquired ingredients for a few recipes for him, and when the book was published, he presented us with a signed copy.

George Harrison lived locally, and also regularly used the shop, having an account.

Tony Hicks of the band The Hollies is a longtime customer of Machin's. The band, formed in the 1960s, is still touring today in 2024.

Jeremy Paxman, who was regularly on TV, had an account, as did Nigel Havers who would come in occasionally.

Two other famous chefs, Anthony Worrall Thompson and Heston Blumenthal also came into the shop. Anthony was a regular customer and Heston called in, as one of his development chefs was often buying from us.

Matthew Fort, the food writer and critic was a regular for many years. He was a collaborator on the 'Food Heroes' television series, also hosted by Rick Stein, which is, we believe, why we were mentioned in the Food Heroes book following the series. Matthew Fort was also a food and drink editor for the Guardian for at least fifteen years. We had a reporter from the Guardian visit us, who authored a wonderful full-page article on Colin and Gabriel Machin. Matthew Fort's mother was also a regular customer. I always enjoyed meeting her, and Tom Fort, Matthew's brother (also an author) lives locally and still regularly shops in Machin's.

We met Mary Berry at one of the food shows. She was so impressed with our food that she became a regular customer. We, in turn, started stocking her salad dressings, as they were superb.

I remember one Saturday when the shop had just closed there was a knock on the shop door. When I opened it, a man was standing there. He said, "I hear you smoke fish; can you smoke these for me?" The man handed me a bag containing three large trout.

After taking contact details I found out the gentleman was Ross Brawn, who was the technical director of the Benetton Formula One racing team. Subsequently, Ross now has an account at Machin's and has for years.

Many customers who come through the door at Machin's are not in the regular sense celebrities, but that isn't to say they are any less interesting or valued, far from it. All the customers shopping at Machin's do so because the shop sells top-quality produce, and the quality justifies the cost.

The wife of John Piper, the artist, used to shop with us. She had a wonderful name 'Myfanwy' and came into Machin's regularly. She was a highly intelligent lady; she knew about her food, and I enjoyed serving her a lot.

There was always a little humour in Machin's, and if a customer was the originator of that, so much the better. One example was Pauline Fleming, with her wonderful northern humour, who delighted in making us think our prices were exorbitant, and that she was not entirely happy, particularly when we told her the joint of rolled rib was twenty-five pounds. She would start with a quick intake of breath, along with a questioning "Really?" but then say, "Oh, wrap it up." If she thought you were trying to be quicker than her in the humour department, she would shoot you down in flames with very few words! She has been a very loyal, longstanding customer for years. I don't know if it's because my father came from Liverpool, but I enjoy that northern humour.

Dorothy Simmons, another humourous lady, had a bit of mischief about her. She would joke about Machin's being in a local paper, typically saying "Oh, were they short of news this week", particularly if it was Barry. Sadly, Dorothy is no longer with us. Everyone at Machin's enjoyed meeting her.

Mark Woodward, whose father is internationally famous, became a regular. He's an interesting, appreciative, regular guy who I've enjoyed meeting for many years now.

Jamie Cassidy was another customer I had a good relationship with. We'd often meet, and he'd greet me as 'Terence'. He's a big seafood fan and liked me to prepare squid etc. I've heard he's quite a good chef. Another customer who enjoys living near the river and still gets out on his boat.

I realised I'd been serving Mark and Linda Compton for at least forty-two years, which I found amazing. Good Lord, we were young forty years ago! Mark is another lover of the Thames, kept busy as a rowing coach, and he still is!

We've had the privilege of serving thousands of loyal and supportive customers over the years. We couldn't have done it without their interaction and interest.

Those mentioned are just a snippet of the thousands I could have chosen.

Chapter

9

Creation

By the mid-1980s we had added an ever-expanding range of cheeses and charcuterie, fresh fish, and a smokehouse, producing our own smoked salmon, and an impressive range of meats. We always wanted to improve our products; our quality and integrity always being paramount. As our knowledge grew our products upgraded, and our supplier confidence influenced buying.

An abattoir in the Scottish Highlands approached us, 'Grants of Dornoch' who would supply us directly, resulting in our ability to source extremely good, consistent quality, beef from a larger stock than the market could produce, and traceability was guaranteed.

Sadly, Grants were only able to supply us for a few years, as the transport was costing more than anticipated and couldn't continue, however, they did put us in touch with another supplier who would be able to supply us with a comparable quality of beef. Prize-winning show beef was often purchased at Christmas. Yes, it was expensive, but was a fabulous advert for the business.

We continued to use a local supplier for some produce. A local producer may phone us to say they had a good side of beef we may be interested in. Usually, these sides of beef were from mature animals, and often very large!

I never enjoyed carrying 1/4 of beef, as physically I wasn't up to it and never really grasped the technique, but Colin always enjoyed the challenge. He kept a record of the heaviest quarter side he had carried and wrote it up on the passage wall. If memory serves me well, I believe one quarter weighed 240 pounds, a crazy weight!

I remember one time we had a side delivered and the delivery man asked me to help him. We got the quarter off the hook and down on the back of the lorry. The carrier suggested I should just 'tip' the piece slowly over, onto his shoulder, and then he said I should follow him into the fridge, to hook it up. Well, I couldn't tip it slowly enough because of its weight, and before I knew it the delivery man and the beef were both on the ground! It took three people to lift it off him and carry it into the fridge. Thankfully, the delivery man was found to be uninjured and recovered after a few minutes.

In the mid to late 1980's the country (under the premiership of Margaret Thatcher) had been experiencing difficult times, however, she was able to counter inflation, thus initiating a recovering economy which helped to create jobs; on top of that we won a victory in the Falklands War. These combined events created a great 'feel good' factor. Many people benefited from the measures created by the government, and having a boost to their finances was very welcome. Consequently, the retail sector experienced a boom time, with plenty of money on the High Street; Machin's felt that too. Our queue was full of dopamine-fuelled customers! We noticed people who might have purchased beef topside as a Sunday roast were now buying rib or sirloin, and we were selling more fillet steak than ever before.

Calves' liver on its own was outselling pigs and lamb liver together, despite the much-increased price.

Although we were still using the Wiltshire supplier, we started to cure more of our gammons and bacon, as Colin wished to produce bacon superior to that generally available, most of which was pumped full of water, nitrates, phosphates, etc. So, he set about researching cures, coming up with the basic cure we'd apply dry. It contained salt and nitrate (at very low levels) which enabled us to produce water-free bacon, which we were extremely proud of.

Salmon was all smoked in Colin's smokehouse. We initially smoked our gammon in there too, however, it wasn't going to cope with the demand, so Colin bought another smoker, specifically for gammon and bacon. This contained a heater, which meant we could now experiment with other things, like duck breasts, whole chickens and breasts, quail, pheasants, trout, and eels, as they were all hot smoked. Consequently, Colin had to buy a refrigerated display cabinet to accommodate everything!

We also smoked our 'Cambridge' pork sausages, and when ready for sale we would hang a string in the shop, which smelt wonderful! I enjoyed cooking a couple of sausages, slicing them up, then eating them in a warm croissant.

The meat trade has product shows and competitions all around the country; producers enter their sausages, pies, bacon, hams, and other goods for judging. Colin was keen to enter some of his products. So, our smoked and unsmoked bacon, Cambridge sausages, along with his pork and leek ones were entered in the 'East of England' show. The smoked back bacon and Cambridge sausages were both awarded gold medals, with the other produce scoring a 'Highly Recommended'! This was the start of our competition journey, and I have to say we were very successful! One was in Harrogate – 'The National Sausage Competition'. We drove there and back in one day.

The sausages had to be cooked immediately before entering, so Lilian cooked them at four in the morning! Colin gave Colin Lovering a lift, as he'd recently bought the Gilbride Shop in Hart Street. Colin Lovering joked, saying if he didn't win, he hoped Colin didn't either!

Colin heard there was going to be a food exhibition in the Olympic Hall, London, so he decided we should have a stall there.

Clive Duncan is one of Gabriel Machin's customers and a near neighbour of Colin. A very well-known artist agreed to paint a backdrop for our show stall, featuring Gabriel Machin's shop, Henley Bridge, and Saint Mary's church. He did a wonderful job.

The show was for three days, so we spent a week or more preparing huge amounts of stock, smoked salmon, bacon, and hams. I was chosen to accompany Colin there. Each day was very busy, but great fun. Mary Berry's daughter had a stall near ours. Shortly after this event, Mary came into the shop, and we started selling the dressings I mentioned earlier.

The stall next to ours was a baker called 'DeGustibus', based in Abingdon. They had amazing bread, which started me on another journey of discovery. DeGustibus is now considered to be the best baker in Britain.

Many customers at the show asked how they could buy our products, as they weren't local to Henley. Consequently, we started a mail-order business on the strength of this request, which grew at subsequent shows we attended, like the NEC, etc. The mail-order smoked salmon was to prove extremely popular, particularly at Christmas, with customers buying for many years.

Anthony Worrall Thompson was making his name as a chef and presenter on the BBC food and drink program. He became a very friendly customer, particularly with Colin. He helped considerably during late-night shopping, as I mentioned. We had a film crew for an entire day in the shop on several occasions, recording material for his program.

The shop regularly gained recognition for the quality and diversity of our produce, along with its knowledgeable staff. We were recommended by the Guide to Good Food Shops in 1979 and 1981, The Good Food Directory in 1984, The Guardian Sausage Directory in 1994, The Guardian Food and Drink in 1998 and featured on BBC food and drink programs.

In 1989 Colin asked if I would take on more responsibility for running the business, as he had a project to start which took him away from the shop, and could only help at weekends, or at very busy times. I was to be in control of all stock orders, the day-to-day workings of stock preparation, monitoring pricing, cleaning, etc. At this time, we had three other members of staff and Lilian no longer served customers but did some office work.

I took a stock count every two weeks with Lilian, who gave me details of how we were doing financially. After the first year under my charge, the shop made a very healthy profit, and I was well rewarded.

Colin lost his wife, and his three boys (Christopher, Daniel, and Nicholas) lost their mum, and I lost a sister when Linda sadly died in January 1995. This was an extremely hard, emotional time for all of us. Many customers who met Linda during her time in the shop offered support and many letters of sympathy. Linda, as well as a very proud Mum, was very supportive of Colin and the business, often involved at Christmas (as previously mentioned) with refreshments for customers waiting to pick up their orders, or cooking and glazing hams, which she was always brilliant at preparing; if we were expecting to work very late in the evenings Linda would bring food for us.

Henley Regatta week was often very busy; we would cook and dress a whole salmon, maybe as many as 30. Linda would help with those when she wasn't watching her boys rowing. All three boys attended Shiplake College, and all had rowed at the Regatta. Daniel continued rowing when he had finished his education, as he was a talented oarsman, finding success several times on final's day at the regatta. I always thought that had he been of larger stature he would surely have gone on to represent his country in senior competitions.

Some customers' sons also rowed, and one was in the 'GB 8', who won gold at the Sydney Olympics. Christopher had a good friend who was also part of that crew.

The river and boats were prominent in their lives. Colin had a cabin cruiser, so we had staff evenings on the river, with Linda preparing food for everyone.

I remember on one outing Colin had arranged to pick up one of the shop suppliers from Hambleden Lock, and when he attempted to get on board the boat drifted out from the bank. We just caught him before he fell in the river!

Chapter

10

Environmental Health

An Environmental Health Officer would, from time to time, call on the business. They would arrive unannounced and check how clean the premises were and would watch you, looking at your work practices.

In the 1960s and 1970s, we only sold meat, so if the EHO called we would quickly look around the premises, making sure all looked tidy. Thankfully, they wouldn't be present for long and would give us a clean bill of health and be on their way.

As our product range grew so did our obligations, health-wise. Colin had to provide hand washing facilities in the shop area and the prep room, plus weighing scales for cheese and cooked meats. Details of any products we cooked on the premises had to be recorded and a cleaning schedule had to be written up, which I know Colin was never in favour of because, as he often said, we worked, we cleaned up, so why would we have to tell anybody that?

In time the amount of paperwork for recording grew and grew, and so did the amount of time the EHO was present, checking everything. They had to tick all the correct boxes though, as that was what was required at the time. We did understand.

The products we vacuum packed had to have a date for 'use by' noted on them. I know Colin spent a small fortune sending products (particularly smoked salmon) to a laboratory for analysis, allowing us to put our claimed shelf life on the labelling.

The problem we found with EHO's was consistency, or the lack of it. One may call and give you five stars and the next one to call finds an issue with your practices, which hadn't changed since the last inspection, and then only reward us 3 stars!

One issue highlighted by the EHO concerned a chicken liver mousse we were selling. It was made in France and one which we'd sold for many years. The problem was that it arrived from France in a 1.5 kg tub, so we had to create smaller portions. The label on the tub stated, 'Once opened, consume rapidly'. We never had any issues regarding longevity, but we had to remove it from sale because we couldn't guarantee its shelf life. I have to say I agreed with their decision on this one product, as we really couldn't guarantee its shelf life. It also proved this specific supplier's disdain for regulations!

Chapter 11

Environment

The world wars had a devastating effect on our ability to produce food, with rationing continuing long after the end of the Second World War.

The UK population boomed between 1945 and 1955, consequently, the farming community (whether arable or livestock) had to respond, increasing production and the methods used, thus obtaining a greater yield.

It may be easy for me to speak after the event, particularly with my limited knowledge, but I do believe the farming community played a significant role in the health of our environment, through my understanding of their mindset and emphasis at the time, and in the decades that followed.

Please don't think I'm being hypocritical of our farmers, as I have great admiration for them. After all, they enabled me to earn a living. I've supported them all my working life, and still do so. I believe farmers responded brilliantly to food shortages, helping to get the country back on its feet after the wars, but some consequences were not apparent at the time.

The use of pesticides has become much more widespread and is now acknowledged as a contributing factor to the scarcity of some bird species today. Bees have suffered from a lack of wildflowers to harvest, and the runoff into water courses has been detrimental to all manner of wildlife.

I do concede some pesticides are necessary with regulation, farming being a difficult vocation financially, as well as manually. In an ideal world, all food produced would be organic, free from any foreign body, and affordable for all, but that seems simply impossible; for a start, there are just too many of us in this world!

In the 1960s and 1970s, some farmers raising beef cattle turned away from their traditional breeds, such as Aberdeen Angus and Hereford, because they're smaller animals, and started breeding larger, European breeds, such as Charolais or Belgian Blue, which yielded a huge amount of meat, resulting in a better reward, financially.

I know there was a lot of talk within the butchery trade about animal feeds containing growth promoters or routine antibiotics that had the same effect.

The food trade was rocked in the 1990s by the BSE scandal. I say scandal because it should never have happened. Creutzfeldt-Jacob Disease is a rare, degenerative brain disorder that affects approximately one in a million people per year. There is no known cure for this. CJD is known as a 'prion' disease, whereby healthy brain tissue deteriorates into an abnormal protein that the body is unable to break down. Animals, as well as humans, can be infected.

In the 1990s the UK had an epidemic of Bovine Spongiform Encephalopathy, BSE, which is a variant of CJD. The symptoms appeared consistent with CJD, and this new form of the illness was found to be contracted by exposure to beef that was contaminated with CJD.

One theory as to why high numbers of cattle were infected was the fact that it had become common practice for dead animals to be processed into the food chain and fed to the cattle.

In humans, the symptoms of CJD usually appear from the age of 60 onwards, so the authorities decided that all beef animals for the food chain must not be older than 30 months when slaughtered, and beef on the bone must not be offered for sale.

Slaughtering processes were changed to ensure no trace of the spinal cord was left in carcasses when delivered out to customers. The control measures put in place were to prevent potentially infected tissues from entering the human food chain, and the measures have been very effective.

Mad cow disease (as BS became commonly known) has thankfully been eradicated; the chance of becoming infected is extremely remote, but it must be remembered that it's extremely likely man created the variant.

Consequently, butchers did experience a downturn in beef sales as customers' confidence in the food trade took a hit which was not unexpected.

The beef we were offering at Machin's was bred in the Scottish Highlands. It was grass-fed, and their winter feed was made up by the farmers themselves. The incidents of BSE in those areas were much lower than in other areas of Britain.

Food scares such as BSE (and to some extent foot and mouth disease, which hit livestock farmers in 2001) do affect customer confidence, but if you can prove the traceability and welfare standards of the produce you're offering, you can dispel customers' fears. I believe the food scares invariably do good, as they have made people look closely at how our food is produced, and only now starting to look at the cost to our environment.

Our relationship with the environment unquestionably must change, particularly the way we produce food, where the plant or muscle has been, with little thought for future implications. Our abuse of land and sea has been shocking.

Currently, in 2024, there is a growing number of people extolling the virtues of a vegetarian or vegan diet and calling for the cessation of animal farming. It's not surprising to tell you I am not one of them! However, I do acknowledge and support their right to choose, whether their conviction is based on moral, environmental, or health grounds.

I do firmly believe that a balanced diet with 'meat and plant' in the correct proportions is what is best for our bodies, but I also believe many of us eat too much, and sometimes the wrong things. I support farmers of all forms, but it must be in harmony with the environment, or it shouldn't be done.

Consumerism has had a bigger effect on our planet than food production, as it can be no coincidence that within most consumer-fuelled societies the population is getting fat and sicker; mentally and physically, plus filling more land, polluting the planet and then spending much more money trying to correct the problems.

We are constantly fed facts of ways to correct the damage we have done to the environment, but many of us are hypocrites, we make very little effort to change our ways. A 'bag for life' that we fill with shopping will not make much of an impact. Many years ago, a 'buy locally' movement failed due to the seduction of stronger marketing strategies.

I bought a diesel car because I was told it was cheaper to run and better than petrol for the environment but now discovered that it isn't. I am not completely convinced about electric cars either. The politicians may tell us we have achieved 'net zero' but I am struggling to believe it can happen within the timescale set out for it.

When we finally take the massive steps needed to repair our planet, I wonder what our food production methods might involve. Possibly our celebrity chefs will all be laboratory technicians, and our food choices will be lab-grown beef steaks, chicken breasts, or salmon fillets, for those who can afford them, and everyone else will have two pills per day, each containing all the vitamins needed to maintain a healthy body, totalling no more than 600 calories each, as to avoid us getting fat. Eat your heart out Heston Blumenthal! The chefs will tell us all yarns of when we farmed animals and grew crops to manufacture our food. Just imagine the effort needed to produce food for everyone!

If I had the opportunity, I would like to say to them, "Thank God I was there!" when food was an exciting voyage of discovery.

Chapter 12

To catch a thief!

Most customers are affable, friendly, and polite, going about their shopping in a manner that you expect, but just occasionally one may surprise you with their actions.

Once, I think in the very early 1980s, we had a surplus of turkeys after Christmas and decided to sell them at a reasonable price, instead of sitting in the freezer for months. A lady came in to buy a turkey, and in those days Molly, our cashier, took the payment. On this occasion the shop was extremely busy with customers and there was quite a queue waiting to pay. This 'lady' took this opportunity to just walk out without paying, and nobody realised until it was too late. The customer knew what she was doing, an opportunity thief!

We had a regular, elderly lady who shopped with us weekly. She often stood, admiring the cheese we had on sale. She used to stand there whilst we were serving the other customers. One week we saw this lady help herself to our Bosciola olives! So, from that point on, every time she came in, we watched her like a hawk! I have to say she was very clever at it and always managed to take several olives without us seeing her, so we christened her 'Olive'. We once offered her a small pot of olives, however she declined, as she obviously enjoyed the challenge!

One day the CCTV installed in the shop picked up the actions of an elderly gentleman, who had been acting suspiciously. He was seen to have slipped a pie in his bag. We spoke to him and let him off with a warning, telling him that if he was seen trying anything like that in the future he would be barred from the shop. We knew he wasn't a poor man, and could pay for his shopping, so we wondered what his motivation was to resort to stealing.

Very early one Saturday morning Barry and I were in the shop waiting for customers to arrive. A young chap came in and was looking around for something ready to eat, he looked as though he had been up all night. He was standing near some packs of biltong when he suddenly grabbed one and ran out of the shop. Barry raced out after him and caught him a little way up the street. Several minutes later I heard the thief had injured his nose on Barry's forehead somehow!

Smoked salmon packs are displayed in an open cabinet where customers can choose for themselves. On one occasion I observed a lady put a pack in her bag, then two minutes later came up to the counter and ordered several meat items. I totalled up her bill and informed her of the amount and said, "That doesn't include the smoked salmon", whereupon the lady said, "Oh my goodness, yes, I had forgotten that!" Was she trying it on? I think yes, she was.

A table sits outside of Machin's, which displays our charcoal, kindling, eggs, and bread, and if anyone wanted to help themselves, they probably could. We did, however, regularly end up with an odd number of eggs! One day a customer told us that he'd just seen a man steal some eggs and looking out of the shop window we could still see him, sitting in the Marketplace, so Barry confronted him and told him, "We know what you've been doing, don't let it happen again or you will be in trouble!" So thankfully that was the end of that problem, or perhaps he had heard about the biltong thief and liked his nose the way it was!

I sold sacks of charcoal outside my shop in Wallingford (which I mention in a later chapter) and one day I watched a young chap pick up a sack, and instead of going into the shop to pay he started to walk off with it! I was going to confront him when I could see he was suddenly aware of me watching him, so he dropped the charcoal in the middle of the pavement and walked very quickly away.

I am very confident all those people mentioned would possess funds to pay for goods, so what is it that motivated them to steal? I am also very confident that there have been many occasions when people have helped themselves to goods that we're unaware of.

Chapter 13

All change

Colin decided he wanted to sell the business. This came as a big shock to me, however, when I considered the very many years he'd worked, plus the long hours he'd put in, along with the changes in his personal life, I completely understood his decision.

Colin did everything he could to help me purchase the business. His accountant drew up a financial plan and we tried to find another staff member, as we'd lost an employee the previous year.

My circumstances were sadly not ideal at that time to take over the business, even though I had the funds. My marriage had broken up and the subsequent divorce was tough and affected me and my confidence to such an extent it wasn't a viable option at that time. It was also proving extremely difficult to attract staff.

Colin understandably felt it was important that any buyer continue in the same vein, trading with the same ethos he had fostered. Had I grasped the opportunity Colin would have been happy, safe in the knowledge I would do this, but it wasn't to be. Finding a buyer with the same food passion, the same commitment to quality, working to the same ethos and being able to not only sustain the business but maybe take it forward, was a massive ask.

Any purchaser of a business considers its financial potential and has no sentimental tie to it; forged over many years. The initial emotion felt by a buyer is the knowledge that they will be parting with a substantial amount of cash, and maybe excitement for the work ahead.

Ian Blandford became the owner of Gabriel Machin in 2003, and although he had been successful in the butchery business before, I think it is fair to say he had a voyage of discovery ahead of him. At that time, he had little knowledge of fish smoking, and cheese. Time and application soon remedied that!

My knowledge of fish and cheese ensured that I carried on the whole side ordering, and Ian dealt with the meat and everything else.

I had always been the 'front of house' so to speak and had a good rapport with many customers. I'm sure the early days of Ian's ownership were at times frustrating, not knowing customers when staff members did, but to his credit, he spent most of his working day serving in the shop and introducing himself to his customers.

Salmon smoking was still one of my tasks, and Ian liked to observe, learning all the time. On one occasion he wanted to see more smoke in the chamber, so he opened the fire box to accomplish this, however, this increased the temperature far too much, the result of which was cooked fish and not smoked. We had plenty of salmon pate for the next few weeks!

The shop had been short of staff for quite a time, consequently, we were missing out on trade. Finding staff locally was very difficult. Ian managed to find some temporary staff, enabling us to get through his first Christmas, plus Richard Mackie (who had worked at Machin's for years) helped for a week, taking time out from his main job. We just about coped, but desperately needed permanent staff.

Barry Wagner came to work with us in 2004 and made a great difference immediately. He worked hard and although he knew nothing about fish or its preparation, picked it up quickly. Bacon curing and smoking, along with sausage making, became his regular weekly tasks. Anthony Worrall Thompson had introduced us to the Guards Polo Club and when a new chef arrived there to run it, we started receiving large orders from them. Barry lived near the club, so he delivered to them on the way home.

Ian picked up one or two other catering contracts which increased our trade quite a bit, which was very welcome. I have to say I enjoyed working with Barry, not only did he work well, but we had lots of laughs together. I was however under more scrutiny and less freedom with Ian than I'd experienced under Colin's management. This is in no way meant as a criticism, as I understandably had to give Ian reasons to be confident in me and build trust between us. I knew this shouldn't present any problems.

Lucas Janczarski came from Poland to find work in England. He had a wife and a very young son at home; he wanted to earn money, giving them a better life than was possible when he worked in Poland. I couldn't have been more impressed with him. I thought he was making huge sacrifices in doing so. Lucas had a poor command of the English language but was very intelligent and able to learn quickly. I worked regularly with Lucas and taught him how to dress and cook salmon, and how to slice a side of smoked salmon (with an electric trimming knife) and then put it into small packs.

Lucas told us that in Poland he'd worked in mechanics and maintained machinery, plus had skills using a personal computer. These skills helped us in the shop enormously, becoming a very valued member of staff. I enjoyed working with Lucas. We talked a lot, and he learned some English, and I in turn learned some Polish. He told me 'Good Morning' was 'Dzien Dobry' in Polish.

Ian never added any new products to the business, as he wasn't the foodie that Colin was, however, he improved the refrigeration, put in a new walk-in freezer, and new deli fridge, plus refurbished the main meat fridge. Machinery was replaced when needed, as the shop had to look tidy, and the window had to be kept well stocked. We always had to be on our toes with that.

Paul Bailey owned 'Bailey's Butchers' shop (previously Appletons) in Duke Street. He decided to sell up, which I thought surprising, as that left Machin's as the only butcher in town, down from seven when I first came to Henley.

Peter Sharp, Gary Heath, and Paul Bailey at Baileys' Butchers

Machin's gained a few customers because of this closure. I thought the town could support two butchers, but the shop reopened as a deli, so at least it was food-related, not coffee or another charity shop!

Chapter 14

Terry 'Two Jobs'

A customer in Machin's told me of a project he was planning. He was the general manager of a company that had two restaurants and was planning for a third. He'd just purchased farmland, within which was a large building that they planned to convert into a farm shop.

They planned to have pigs, which would supply the butchery in the shop. They also planned to have a market garden growing vegetables etc., which would supply the restaurants. Also in the plans was a smoker to be used for their products. All in all, it sounded like a very exciting project!

Henley Standard, September 22nd, 2006 – 'There is one very familiar face missing from Henley town centre this week. After 38 years working at Gabriel Machin's in the Market Place, Terry Colby is moving on. Terry started work at the tender age of 15 and ever since then his smiling face and friendly manner have welcomed a legion of customers. Last weekend saw a little party as he said goodbye to the butcher's shop and hello to the farm shop behind the Crazy Bear pub at Stadhampton where Terry will be keeping himself busy. I wish him well on behalf of everyone in the town.'

The seed was planted in my head, so I decided to have a meeting with the people involved, to try and glean more information about the project.

The upshot of this meeting was being offered the position of manager at the 'Crazy Bear Farm Shop', in Stadhampton, which I was excited to accept.

I gave my notice to Ian and explained my plans and the date I intended to leave Machin's. He took it very well and wished me all the best and said if I thought things were not as I'd hoped I was to call him and discuss returning to my job there.

Przemek Stuba came to work at Machin's in September 2007, two weeks before I left. He was the cousin of Lucas and I found him very personable too. He had some chef experience and would be an ideal member of staff.

The general manager of the Crazy Bear christened me 'Terry Two Jobs', as I was starting my second job 39 years after my first!

My first weeks were spent travelling around, speaking to potential suppliers, getting ready for the building to be completed, plus planning the opening day.

I visited Borough Market in London, which is one of my all-time favourite foodie places, a real food Mecca. The market is rumoured to have existed since the early 12th century, if not earlier! It now sells speciality foods to everyone, having previously only sold to the wholesale market. Borough Market and Covent Garden are the main food markets trading in London. Sellers come from all over the United Kingdom, alongside those who import products from Europe. They sell all sorts of produce, including vegetables, fruit, meat, game, cheeses, pastries and bread.

I introduced myself to 'Brindisa', who imported wonderful Spanish produce. I loved watching the staff carve up their Iberico hams, and whilst doing so they told me about the differences in their age and flavours. As I was a potential customer, I was given a sample, which only served to reinforce what I already believed, that these Spanish hams, where the pigs roamed free and their diet included acorns, coupled with their skill in ageing and curing, produced the finest hams in the world.

Brindisa also sold interesting cheeses, some new to me. Manchego, supplied in various degrees of maturity, Monte Enebro - a goat milk cheese, intense but creamy, and Idiazabal, as sheep milk cheese which is often smoked.

There were often 100 stalls in the market, covered with worldwide produce. It is so enjoyable just to walk around, chatting with the traders, soaking up their infectious enthusiasm and knowledge, and often seeing their expertise and skill firsthand, as they either produce or source the finest foods. I have from a very young age loved dates, and there is a stall there selling nothing but! All of amazing quality; so if you want a good date Borough is the place to go!

On the edge of the market, Neal's Yard Dairy has a shop that I always have to resist. I marvel at the selection and the sheer quality of their cheeses; they are usually generous with giving out samples.

I also found Villanova, a company that specialised in the best that Italy produces; amazing cheeses, a 36-month organic Parmesan Reggiano among them and more Pecorino than I knew existed, plus Mozzarella and Burrata to die for, with a great range of salami. The results of these wonderful tastings and visits meant I had lots of possibilities for the farm shop. A supplier of proper free-range chickens from Essex completed my supplier list.

We opened the farm shop in October 2007, and I was full of vim and vigour, however, I am sad to say things didn't work out as planned. The owner's strategy and mine differed considerably. We were attracting trade, but I considered it not enough.

One highlight was the head chef from Raymond Blanc's 'Manoir', who came in to regularly buy Jabugo ham, which I had hoped may lead to other purchases.

When working for Colin I'd never had any doubts about working conditions, as he was always sincere and could be trusted completely, but recent events taught me I'd been too relaxed, trusting, and a little naive.

The owners increased the opening hours by an hour, so every evening we were open until 7:00 pm, which wasn't what I'd signed up for at all. This, with other incidents, was enough to make me resign.

Chapter

15

Homecoming

I phoned Ian Blandford to arrange an informal chat. He offered me a job, returning to Machin's after I'd completed my notice period at the farm shop.

The lads at the shop gave me a great welcome back. Przemek Stuba aka 'gorgeous' was very personable, and made his presence felt in the shop. He often bought fish now.

Lucas enjoyed his work in the prep room where he was responsible for overseeing a lot of the manufacturing processes, including curing and slicing bacon, smoking gammon, chicken and duck breasts, along with slicing and packing salmon. I had previously taught him these skills, and he seemed to have picked them up quickly, perhaps even faster than I did!

I worked alongside Barry much of the time; we had lots of jokes and funny moments, as our sense of humour, although different, seemed to gel and was often hilarious; Kcab Gnals was often involved. Barry was sometimes accused of being a 'methane man' for obvious reasons and one time just before Christmas the air in the shop was particularly potent and a lady customer walked in the shop, took a huge lungful of air, and said, "I absolutely love the aroma in this shop at Christmas time." She clearly had no inkling as to why we were in fits of laughter.

I made a few great relationships with customers at the farm shop, however, I thoroughly enjoyed being back serving people I had known for many years. I assumed my previous mantle as the cheese buyer, which I of course loved to do.

The website was being revamped and I was extremely pleased when Ian commented on my cheese knowledge, as being almost encyclopedic.

Previous Christmases had always been hard, with long hours worked, but as always, paid overtime was very welcome at an extremely expensive time of the year. However, Ian was preparing some products earlier and earlier, so there was less call for us all to do any overtime.

I recommended some of the products I'd found for the farm shop to Ian, so he ordered from Villa Nova, (the importer of Italian produce) a range of salami, which were of much better quality than those available from the markets we currently used, and cheeses, including La Ter, which is a lovely very soft mixed milk cheese; a buffalo mozzarella and a hard cow's milk cheese, that's washed in red wine while maturing called 'Ubriaco', which translates as 'drunken'. Ian also bought from Mons, Cheesemongers.

The cheeses we sold at Christmas were joined by others we hardly stocked at other times of the year: Tete de Moine, Raclette, and Reblochon included.

A food festival was planned for Henley, so Ian decided we would have a stall there, so I was asked to help serve on the day, selling packs of bacon, smoked salmon, and sausages.

Jose from a company called 'Delicioso' joined us. He was giving out tasters of his 'Iberico' ham, which we started to stock at the shop, as well as other products he was importing.

The festival was in the centre of the town, with a large marquee in the marketplace, within which chefs advertised their business and produce. Paul Clerehugh from the Crooked Billet was cooking venison burgers. I'd previously thought they were something we could be selling at the shop. Chefs were also giving talks and demonstrations in the town hall, Raymond Blanc amongst them.

All in all, I thought it was a great idea, as a showcase for local businesses, and hoped it may be a yearly event. I also thought that the space available in the marketplace may not be sufficient if it proved very successful.

Sadly, things didn't work out for me on my return. Initially, we all worked well together, however, I felt undervalued and my passion for our products and foods didn't seem to be shared with those it should have been, consequently I knew I had to move to somewhere this would be appreciated.

Chapter

16

Terry goes walkabout (Dagayu)
Food discovery through travel

My holidays are often planned with local food opportunities in mind, with markets high on the list, whether permanent indoor markets or temporary stalls in the street, I love them all. The fish market in Venice for example, along with the fruit and vegetable street stalls were impressive.

The Mercato di Sant Ambrogio is a fresh food market in Florence. It has souvenirs outside and food inside. The meat quality is impressive, with very good butchers, and many bakers making brilliant quality breads.

Mahon in Menorca had a very interesting market, thankfully with many locally made goods, which isn't always the case.

I found a street market in Croatia and their selection and quality of fruit was stunning, why do we not get food like that at home?

French markets are legendary. I visited Avignon and sampled some excellent cheese and wine in the covered markets like Les Halles. I'm always amazed at the stores selling spices, herbs, and salts. I watched a meat stall where young butchers were preparing cuts for display and was interested to see their different techniques, compared to how we portion meats at home. There was a huge Sunday outdoor market, where you could buy everything and more. If you have experienced a real French market, then the ones at home claiming to be French are disappointing.

My repertoire in the kitchen expanded hugely when I met my wife Jeannette, who is from South Africa, but spent much of her life in Italy, Sardinia in particular.

Paella is a dish that's eaten at Christmas in Sardinia, and Jeannette introduced me to it and makes it often, which is wonderful. I even came to terms with the texture of mussels that I'd previously struggled with.

Jeannette had been taught to make pasta and risotto in Italy. I had eaten both but never cooked either at home. 'Spag bole' was about as far as I'd got, however, we were now having a risotto every week and making our pasta. Sometimes, if there was a little pasta dough left over, Jeannette would deep fry some and sprinkle it with icing sugar when cooled; it tasted great. She said it was called 'Chiara', but I have also seen it called 'Acciuleddi'. We also make our pizzas from scratch, equally as good as any I have tasted in Italy.

Being very English, I enjoy winter dishes and comfort food. Tartiflette is a fabulous cold-weather dish we enjoy, made with Reblochon cheese. Just the mention of it conjures up thoughts of snow-covered mountains and people skiing. I have never been skiing but I had to try Tartiflette! It's a dish from Savoy in the French Alps and Aosta Valley. It is made with potatoes, Reblochon cheese, lardons, and onions. A splash of white wine can be added too.

South Africa

Jeannette's father had died, so we went to South Africa for the funeral. We stayed with her aunt who made a real 'braai' (barbecue) when we were there. The starters were Biltong and a beer, followed by fabulous quality steak, costing about half the price of those at home.

We watched the South African Springboks team play at Newlands in Cape Town, and all along the road to the stadium there were stalls selling Boerewors rolls, Droewors (dried sausage), and of course Biltong. It was an acquired taste, but I wouldn't miss it now. The food in South Africa is very good quality; the seafood was great, and their fish and chips surprisingly, were as good as any at home.

View from the family home at Betty's Bay in the Western Cape

Whilst visiting South Africa Jeannette wanted to meet up with family and friends she'd not seen for a long time. Her cousin Frank kindly offered to put us up at his house, planning to take us on a bit of a tour to see some of the country. Frank lives in the Western Cape area, so it's a wonderful spot to be based as his house is right by the sea where we could spot seals and dolphins from his living room. The beautiful sunsets were amazing, nearly every evening.

**Stunning sunset from the family home
Betty's Bay**

We set off on our travels, driving part of the 'Garden Route', which takes you up country, planning to travel through Karoo on the return. The morning we set off Frank suggested we should stop for breakfast at a parade of shops. He knew where there was a café we might find interesting.

Garden Route – South Africa

We pulled into a nearby car park close to a barbeque where three ladies were baking what appeared to be bread. I chatted with them, and they told me they were making and cooking 'Roosterkoek' which looked like large baps with a texture similar to pitta bread.

When cooked, the Roosterkoek would be split open and filled with an amazing variety of fillings, from cheese, ham, spicey minced beef, and cooked meats to fruit and jams. It would be eaten any time from breakfast to supper time. The ladies were very proud of what they were cooking, telling me the flour was local and stone ground, so my choice for breakfast was Roosterkoek with cheese and ham.

Travelling along the coast we stopped at several beautiful spots for coffee and early evening we bought fish and chips, eating them by the sea. The variety of fish available was exceptional. You could buy a carton containing fish, calamari, and even prawns. I thought it was a great idea; the quality was excellent.

We continued travelling around the country for three nights and I saw for the first time how beautiful it is, sampling many wonderful local foods on the way. We had Kudu steak one evening, served with a spicy sauce; and lamb shank another evening, also with spices, showing how the influx of Asian people influenced the foods.

Bester Biltong Butchers
Orange Free State Province - South Africa

We stopped at a butcher's Frank knew who specialised in Biltong and Droewors. I chatted to them about the cuts of meat used for Biltong. I made biltong myself and used beef silverside, as do most people in England because of the cost, but this chap told me he used silverside, topside, and even rump steak, which I could identify as they were hanging in the shop. The lamb he was selling came from the Karoo and looked great quality, which I find surprising, as that area is very dry with less vegetation than other regions. He had a variety of beef, some of which was very good. Hardly any fat covering, however, that may have been used for Biltong or Boerewors sausages.

Whilst travelling I couldn't see any markets, or anything I could define as a market, however, there were several large farm stores we stopped to look in, none of which had a variety of meats, but all had an amazing amount of honey alongside jars of chutneys, cooked vegetables, preserves, and confit, which is usually fruits in syrup.

There were many wine farms and Frank had arranged for us to have a tasting at one close to home called 'Villion', which was a great experience. The wife of the owner hosted the tasting; she really knew her products and we did buy a few bottles naturally!

Villion Wine Estate - Western Cape, South Africa

The Villion family were originally from France and had been in Africa since the 1600s. I would've liked to visit the Muratie Wine Estate, as it's owned by the Melck family. I'd known Deon and Jill Melck well as customers at Gabriel Machin for very many years, but sadly time didn't allow for that. Deon had been an agent for a company selling excellent quality knives. Many years beforehand we had given him butchery lessons at Machin's, teaching him how to butterfly a leg of lamb.

I looked for cheese everywhere in all the food shops I went into, but I could never find any local, home-produced cheeses of the standard we are used to at home. The only store I found selling continental cheese was Woolworths, which are their equivalent of Marks and Spencer.

Florence Market

I'd always wanted to visit Florence, so we set off, as I'd heard The Mercato Centrale was the largest permanent market in the city, and a must-see, situated in a wonderful historic building, and spread over two floors, with much of the upper floor housing many local eateries offering cooked foods. I stood and watched a chef carve from a wild boar he was roasting on a spit - I had to try some, along with the porchetta he was cooking. He told me the porchetta had been made from a whole pig he'd boned out, with stuffing in the middle which included the liver and some herbs, such as fennel, which is an ingredient I like with pork. I could easily detect that in my portion.

Some of the meat stalls sold tripe or 'trippa' as the Italian people called it, which used to be quite popular in England, but now has been rejected by all but the older shoppers. Most of Europe still finds tripe an attractive meat. The butcher told me people usually cook it in a sauce including chopped tomatoes, sometimes with Parmigiano grated on the top. Lucas from Machin's once made me some soup containing tripe, which is very popular in Poland.

The second-floor eateries were mostly selling Italian foods like pasta and pizza, but you could buy a Florentine beef steak that came with roasted potatoes, or sausages, also with potatoes and salad. There were burgers available, which I found a bit sad. I know they are very popular, but personally, I would like a good quality food court to be traditional, and burgers were not a traditional food in Italy. I did see a kitchen selling Chinese-style foods, so I suppose you have to cater to all tastes.

On the ground floor, they sold meats, cheeses, vegetables, and bread, along with mushrooms, both fresh and dried. Most of the chickens for sale were very yellow, probably corn-fed, and many ready for cooking, whereas in previous years they would have had their heads and feet intact to be prepared later.

The fruit and vegetables all looked to be of fantastic quality, with a large variety available. I was taken with one stall where they sold nothing but tomatoes, and what an amazing variety they had. When I was very young, I didn't eat tomatoes, but I love them now and grow several types every year.

The city wasn't too large so exploring on foot wasn't a problem. Their architecture and the culture has to be seen to be appreciated. Whilst walking I found a baker's shop. It was tiny and could've easily been missed, but my foodie nose found it, and what an amazing find it was. The bread was the work of a real artisan.

Spain – Bilbao

For a long time, I had wanted to visit the Basque region of northern Spain; San Sebastian in particular, because of its fame for their quality of food. I decided we would start our tour in Bilbao. It had shed its image as an industrial area I felt, now becoming appreciated as a fine food area. We also wanted to visit the Guggenheim Museum.

The Guggenheim Museum

Bilbao Food Market, La Ribera

Our hotel was in central Bilbao, so we walked everywhere and sampled the local specialities, including the pintxos, (small finger food) which come in a whole range of toppings: meat, fish (particularly prawns), cheese, vegetables, and even eggs. They are so inventive. I particularly enjoyed the anchovy and peppers, along with cheese and chorizo, but to be honest, there were not many I didn't like.

We visited one or two bars, having a couple of pintxos and a glass of wine; a great way to spend lunch, or an evening, enjoying the atmosphere and ambience, and people-watching at leisure.

I, as usual, wanted to locate the market. We found it in a fabulous area right by the river. We visited early in the morning and found a great many stalls. I thought the range of fish and shellfish was extensive and of great quality. All the fish merchants were on the ground floor, and butchers with meat-related produce on the first floor. The butchers had a lot of sirloin of beef on display, with much of the beef from fairly large animals, quite lean and not much fat compared to how we like to see it at home.

I did try to talk to a few butchers, but I found it surprising that most didn't speak any English, however, I managed to ask one what the breed of cattle was he'd taken the beef from, and he said it was 'Pirenaica', often from milking cows, but they also had young male animals, as they were a popular local breed. Scottish Aberdeen Angus was occasionally in stock he told me.

Hams

The fruit and vegetables were all on the top floor and as always, I found the variety and quality fantastic. There was a cafeteria area with a range of dining options, all of which looked of a good standard, but we didn't eat there, instead opting for a coffee in the café by the river. I thought the market was well laid out and one of the best I had ever visited, along with its great location.

Spain – San Sebastian

After two days in Bilbao, we then travelled to San Sebastian. I couldn't wait to see it for myself after thinking about visiting for such a long time. We had travelled from Bilbao by coach, and I couldn't believe how cheap it was. The 45-mile journey was £7 each, so much less than at home.

The seaward side of San Sebastian is stunning. The beach area known as Playa De La Concha is really beautiful and we walked the promenade, sitting on the beach with some takeaway food, taking in the stunning view.

The old town 'Parte Vieja' is the area I was most interested in visiting, and it certainly didn't disappoint, with its upmarket shops and a myriad of bars and restaurants. The pintxo bars were a step up from any we had already seen. Their inventiveness, their displays, and their sheer quality were magnificent, so we had to experience a few along with a glass or two of Rioja!

The old town was very busy and lively, particularly in the evenings, which created a really warm ambience and a great place to be. It was possible to book a guide who took small groups on a tour of a selection of pintxos bars, but we decided we wanted to explore and find out on our own.

San Sebastian market

We ate at the bars for much of the time and hadn't had what you would call a 'main meal' since arriving in Spain, so we decided on the evening before we left San Sebastian that's exactly what we needed.

We hadn't booked a restaurant, but whilst walking around the old town I saw a restaurant with a great display of beef hanging in the back. It all looked great quality, so we decided to give it a try.

San Sebastian meat market

We went in and sat down. A waiter soon appeared and told us in detail the origins of the beef. I chose a large T-bone steak, large enough for both of us, originally cut from the sirloin of a Spanish mature milking cow, which is very different from what is used at home. I asked the waiter how it was going to be cooked and he explained that they cooked over coals and recommended rare to medium, which is exactly how we like it. The waiter even brought the meat to show me before cooking, which I thought was great. When cooked the steak was taken off the bone, sliced, then arranged on a trivet. It looked fantastic and cooked to perfection. We both agreed we had never had a better steak anywhere. The waiter explained they aimed to achieve maximum flavour and not necessarily the softest steak, but we told him our meal was successful on both counts.

To accompany our steak we had a very simple salad and of course, a glass or two of local vino, as nothing else was needed; a fitting end to our visit to San Sebastian.

We did seek out the local market, but I think we arrived too late in the day, as many stalls were closed and there wasn't a great selection of produce left. Perhaps we shall return another day and give it another chance to impress, and we will try to visit other towns and villages along the coast, particularly Getaria where there are noted restaurants.

Our Spanish holiday ended with two days in Barcelona, which on reflection wasn't long enough to do all the touristy bits we should have; however, we had a great hotel with a nearby square where there was a good bar serving coffee and wine. We sat and watched the people go by, which we always enjoy.

We visited the famous market 'La Boqueria', luckily arriving early, as the crowds grew massively in a short time. I spoke with one trader about the hams and jamon he was selling. He told me the best Pate Negra can cost £400 or more.

Some of the traders were selling small paper cones containing ham, usually Serrano, which is cheaper, but still good quality ham, as well as cheese, mostly Mahon, which we thought was a good snack keeping off the hunger whilst walking around. The volume and selection was impressive although not always of the best quality, but as a spectacle I can see why it attracts the thousands of people it does. I also think that the prices are a little higher there than elsewhere because of its entertainment value and visual spectacle.

Chapter

17

'Two Jobs' continued

I had known Gary Smith for years. He'd wanted to buy Machin's when Colin was selling up. I didn't know any details as to why that didn't happen, however he went on to buy 'The Old Calnan Shop' in Benson.

Gary saw the potential of a butcher's shop in Wallingford, as there hadn't been one there for many years, so he was on the search for suitable premises. Carl Woods was the last butcher in Wallingford. He'd sold his premises to Waitrose, who built their store there. He moved to Sonning Common and built up a good business. Carl would always come to the Wallingford shop to wish us a Merry Christmas.

Gary found somewhere ideal, which strangely, had been a pet shop in a previous life; different animals than he was planning on stocking! He planned to stay in his Benson shop, so he was on the lookout for an ideal person to manage his Wallingford butcher's shop – me!

I was offered a very good salary and the freedom to buy pretty much what I considered we could sell, which in retrospect I think was a mistake on Gary's part because the shops were not aligned enough. I had different ideas about the stock I wished to sell and the clientele I hoped to attract. However, the freedom to buy was great for me, as I was buying sides of beef from the Orkney Islands, which were sometimes organic, and buying from the Speyside supplier, so all beef was top quality with proven provenance.

Steve and I, behind the new 'Tech Z' Cabinet

Pork and lamb were all local and of the quality I needed, plus a range of game, which included wild boar from the Forest of Dean and on occasion goat meat, either from the market or sometimes a local producer, which completed our offerings.

We had a fresh fish counter which was well stocked daily. Our cheese came from my trusted suppliers, Neal's Yard and Mons. We had a large selection, including the local cheese from the Village Maid.

At a later point, when other local cheeses emerged, I started to buy direct from Village Maid, the Barkham Blue from Two Hoots cheeses, and the excellent creations from Rose Grimond at the Nettlebed Creamery.

I also stocked Sinodun Hill, made from the milk of Anglo Neubion goats, made by Fraser Norton and Rachel Yarrow. The cheese looks like a French cheese, Pouligny. The name is derived from the 'Wittenham Clumps', a local landmark.

In retrospect, I probably had too large a selection for our customer base, but I have to say I was enjoying so many cheeses which were new to me! Including Mimolette and Beauvale, a soft, Stilton-like cheese, and a few French goats' cheeses.

I advertised cheeses for special occasions by way of cheese towers for weddings, anniversaries and birthdays, usually involving four or five 'tiers' of cheese. Some of these included local cheese, built from a selection from the customers' personal choice, which proved to be very successful.

I visited a local orchard at Mapledurham. The owner spent quite a long time showing me around and educating me about her apples and pears, which were brilliant. Her fruit was a vast improvement on anything for sale in local supermarkets.

When I left, I took several boxes away with me! Her Cox's Orange Pippins were great. The pears were 'Gleu Morceau', which I'd never heard of beforehand. They were stunning and both sold well in the shop.

The trade was excellent and growing well, but it was very hard work, as a combination of long hours and the travelling time there and back amounted to a long working week. The drive to work in the summer was great, but during the winter, not so much, particularly if snow was on the road. I once got marooned at the shop overnight as the road was closed due to a huge lorry and trailer jack-knifing across the road.

I could cure bacon for myself and knew the Wiltshire company (who I'd known for years through Machin's) would smoke some for me.

Nitrate-free bacon is supposed to be a much healthier option, so I decided to experiment, as there's evidence that processed foods containing nitrates can be carcinogenic and consequently, get bad press because of it. My regular bacon had a very low-level cure, which is quite different from mass-produced foods commonly available in supermarkets.

I bought a book containing a list of E numbers. It confirmed my suspicions, that the purpose of additives was to extend shelf life; there would be many more instances of food poisoning without them. I would urge everyone to get some literature explaining E numbers, if only to find out what additives are in our food. It isn't only processed foods that contain them, the information will surprise you!

Sausages were made to my recipe too; an authentic Italian sausage, the recipe included pork, fennel, garlic, nutmeg, and pepper, with the meat marinated in red wine, which proved to be very successful I'm pleased to say!

My Christmas sausages were a big hit too, containing rosemary, and cranberry. I marinated the pork meat in mulled wine, which the customers found delicious, and asked for throughout the year.

I enjoyed having the freedom to create these lovely foods myself, particularly when I was getting very positive feedback from customers.

Gary Smith and his wife separated, and as his wife owned half of the business things were suddenly up in the air, leaving me uncertain of what may happen. We carried on as normal, however, problems arose which threatened the business, and I was expecting to be out of work.

The Wallingford shop was put up for sale, so I bought it with another member of staff. My motivation was first and foremost that I didn't want to be out of work, however, in retrospect, I probably would have chosen a different path. The partnership wasn't for me.

Customers are the most important and rewarding part of the business, at least in my view, and if you are not personable with people it's a difficult sell. If it's not something you are comfortable with then it's not for you.

I had forged good relationships with many customers and when I announced my intention to move on, they were quite sad but interested to know what the future held for me.

My future wasn't bleak, as there was a possibility of setting up a business with Mario, my stepson, who was a very good chef, but that wasn't guaranteed, although the idea was a very attractive one.

Another possibility arose: a local farm shop wanted me to set up a fresh fish counter, but I had no interest in that. There was also a business acquaintance who wanted to set me up in a business, but I thought it would never be mine, and with my ideas, I could envisage that he would want too much involvement, so I turned him down.

I learned a lot in Wallingford; I made mistakes, but sometimes you must make mistakes to learn. I do think when I went to work in Wallingford, I still had too much of 'Machin's' in my head and tried to set up a 'like for like' business. A major problem was most of the clientele in Wallingford were asking for slightly different produce than those we offered to Henley customers. As a consequence, sadly, we didn't attract enough people. I probably should've altered the strategy, which may have made us more successful than we were.

The two owners of Gabriel Machin since Colin Marett sold up have done an excellent job maintaining the business; creating *the* 'go-to' food shop in the area, improving the premises, and spending a lot of money doing so. However, I always felt something was missing.

Colin was always interested in woodturning and had the time to indulge in that when he retired. I'd heard he was exhibiting at an art show near where we lived, so I went to visit him. When I saw the lovely wooden items he was making, and heard him talking about the wood he was using with such passion, I immediately realised that was what I missed in Machin's, that passion for ingredients. I'm not critical of anyone who doesn't have this passion, as we all make an impact in our way.

Chapter

18

Homecoming (again)

Ian Blandford sold Gabriel Machin to Barry Wagner in 2015, making Ian the proprietor who owned Gabriel Machin for the shortest time.

I had always kept a good friendship with Barry, and he occasionally got me produce from the market for the Wallingford business when I had difficulty sourcing it.

I'd never considered I may ever return to Machin's; however, Barry knew I intended to leave my partnership, and as he'd recently lost one of his staff, offered me a job when I was available. I knew I would only be able to work full-time for the following few years, and it would be great to be back where it all started, 50 years ago.

Firstly, I thought it was a crazy idea, but realised it was where I wanted to be, so said yes! Barry found staff recruitment difficult, as most food manufacturing businesses did. Many businesses advertised through agencies in Europe, particularly Poland. If this hadn't been the case, I wouldn't have had the opportunity to return to my roots! So, I returned, and Barry posted the fact on the Machin Facebook page, where many people responded with lovely positive comments.

It was immediately apparent that the Barry who now owned the business was a different person to the Barry I'd worked with years before. He was much more intense and scrutinised every action staff undertook, which most find hard to take, but you just do a good job and don't let that be a worry. I understood Barry's mindset and accepted it, as having been in similar shoes at the Wallingford shop, I knew why.

Barry wanted me to be responsible for the cheese counter and all the ordering, which I was very pleased to take on, and introduced some cheeses I was selling in Wallingford, like Delice De Bourgogne - a soft cow's milk cheese, which was extremely popular, and Beauvale, a very soft blue cheese made by Cropwell Bishop, who makes an excellent Stilton. I also introduced a Camembert, which is unpasteurised and better quality than the one which was being stocked.

Lucas Janzarski was still working there and oversaw all the manufacturing, curing, and smoking of chicken, duck breasts, and trout, along with making smoked salmon pate, which was even more popular than ever. He also sliced smoked salmon for the retail packs. A very valuable member of staff.

Przemek Stuba aka 'gorgeous' was still employed there and was his usual exuberant self; loud, but very good to work with! He was responsible for the fish counter. Sadly, Przemek's mother-in-law in Poland was in very poor health, so his whole family were making plans to return home permanently, to be closer to the family.

I became reacquainted with many customers I'd known for years and met many new ones. My food knowledge and skills showed the new customers I knew what I was talking about, thus gaining their confidence and trust. I advised them on the variety and size of cheeses they needed for a board, depending on the number of guests and the occasion being catered for, plus how to cook certain fish and meat dishes, creating great customer relations.

When Christmas came Barry oversaw the main cheese order, generally mirroring the previous year's orders, followed by a top-up order from me if needed. I ordered a few individual cheeses I considered would be good to have over the Christmas trade. Barry was a little reluctant to step out from what he knew, as he felt it was a risk not worth taking, not wanting to be left with the stock post-Christmas rush. I was confident (through experience) that we would sell it all, and thankfully we did.

I remember one Christmas a customer ordered a 'Fruit De Mer' for 10 people, and after a brief discussion decided on one large king crab, two dressed crabs, two lobsters, twenty large prawns, and two dozen oysters. The customer contacted us later to tell us how wonderful it all looked within their Christmas display and how pleased they were with everything.

Przemek had moved back to Poland, so I was now ordering most of the fish and preparing the salmon for smoking. I would fillet the fish and cure it all with dry salt overnight, then they would be washed to remove the salt and hung in the smokehouse. Barry would then finish the smoking process.

We heard murmurings of something called 'Coronavirus', and that it was possibly going to be a problem. The reports said it was likely to be like having the flu. Some elderly customers panicked and bought large quantities of food to stock up their freezers. Sadly, soon the news was everywhere of people dying from the COVID-19 pandemic, and shop trade became crazy; we had queues outside the shop all day, every day, with people stocking up, and buying huge quantities.

When the first lockdown was announced we introduced social distancing, with no more than two customers at a time in the shop, the result of which was an even bigger queue – the scene was like the Christmas trading period, and this went on for weeks.

Customers were ringing up wanting to place orders and asking for deliveries, which we couldn't do because we were so busy. Some customers just wanted to pull their car up outside and have us put their order in the boot. Many were shopping with us rather than at their usual supermarket because they were seen as risky places.

I was in an awkward situation because I was classed as vulnerable, owing to my age and medical condition, and my wife has an even more vulnerable condition, so ideally, I would have preferred to be furloughed, but that wasn't possible because of the volume of work, so I had to be extra careful with my hygiene and washing, etc.

Most people were taking Covid seriously, but there was a small element who didn't believe things were as bad as the figures being quoted and acted in quite a blasé manner, particularly with their distancing, etc. We did have several issues with people just walking into the shop with no thought for customers already there. I thought they had a terribly arrogant attitude.

My stepson Mario lost his father-in-law to Covid, so I was always taking it seriously.

The town was very weird, like a ghost town, with most shops closed and most cars on the road coming to our shop!

Two members of staff left. Their departure coincided with the closure of a butcher's shop in Reading. Consequently, their staff needed new positions, so the timing couldn't have been better. They came to work at Machin's, which was great luck for us, as we would never have coped with the volume of work without them. Terry and Denis had worked together for more than twenty-five years, so they were happy to be working together again, so we now had two Terrys on the staff.

Then the second lockdown came, which included the Christmas period. On a normal Christmas, we would've had a queue that may have stretched to 30 yards long, however, this one was around 300 yards long, including distancing, and again, some were not taking things seriously enough sadly. I served one customer who'd just flown in from the USA, and had no concerns at all, which I found surprising, considering how serious the pandemic was in America at that time; he had no mask and didn't distance himself from anyone, along with an awfully selfish attitude.

We found wearing masks whilst working not easy at all, and the Environmental Health Officer made Barry erect some screens in the shop. I think the government's attitude to Covid influenced the general attitude of malaise some members of the public had at that time.

The Prime Minister didn't seem to act with conviction. I couldn't understand the government's decision to give essential businesses awards of money to help them get through the pandemic, when those businesses were experiencing huge hikes in trade and were making more money than normal. I thought the money should've gone to businesses that may not survive because of the pandemic.

The furlough scheme was probably a good idea, but we now know that was open to fraud by some people, as was the bounce-back loan offered.

I have to say I was thoroughly enjoying the time at work with my old friends and forging new relationships with others – all very rewarding, but manual work is tiring, and although I think that kept me fit, I was of course getting older and thought it was about time I slowed down a little.

Cutting my hours at Machin's was sadly not an option Barry could work with, and on chatting to my wife Jeannette we decided I should retire, and that we would be ok. I didn't want to retire completely, as ideally, I would have liked just a few hours a week, however, the more I thought about it the better an idea it became.

I told Barry of my decision the next day and I have to say he took it well. He shook my hand, thanked and congratulated me, then wished me well. I gave him two months' notice, knowing how difficult it is to find staff, particularly someone with experience.

A good friend of mine works at Higgs Group in Henley. They publish the Henley Standard etc. They kindly put a fabulous feature in it about my retirement and intention to write a book detailing a little of my life and journey, much of which was spent at Machin's.

Customers who knew of my retirement were amazing, with many coming in to wish me well. I was taken aback by their generosity of words and gifts. One customer gave me a hamper with champagne and chocolates; I was embarrassed by their attention.

Twenty years after Colin Marett sold the business to Ian Blandford, I'm very pleased to see most of the products and practices are still in place, and very little has changed, which is a huge compliment to all the products and methods we instigated over many years, along with the reputation we gained whilst doing it. Had I been able to buy the business, I may have explored other areas as retail markets changed. Something that we always responded to, if it went hand in hand with our ethos.

I retired officially on 31st March 2022, almost 54 years after starting work; 44 years of that spent in Machin's. I doubt anyone has ever worked there longer.

A few of Terry's favourite recipes…

Terry's Fish Pie

Recipe:

(for 4 people – no potato recipe)

600 g of natural smoked haddock
200 g cod fillet
200 g salmon
One block of puff pastry
2 eggs
50 g of butter
50 g of plain flour
100 g of cheddar - grated
500 g milk

Method:

Place all the fish in a large saucepan filled with cold water. Poach until boiling, then turn off the heat.

Roll out the pastry to fit a rectangular baking tray.

Hard boil the eggs and cool them down.

Flake all the fish and carefully mix, spreading it along the base of the pastry.

Peel the eggs and slice them, laying the slices all over the top of the fish.

Make a roux with the butter and flour, then add the milk, constantly stirring until the mix is spooning consistency.

Add the cheese and keep stirring until the cheese has melted and the mixture is smooth.

Season the fish and eggs with salt and pepper then carefully cover the fish with the sauce using a spoon.

Carefully wrap the pastry up and around the pie.

Baking at 200C (180C Fan) Gas Mark 6 for approximately 24 minutes until the pastry is golden and serve with asparagus or savoury rice.

Terry's Shin of Beef Pie

Recipe:

(for 4 people)

800 g diced shin beef, large pieces
1 small onion, finely chopped
200 g smoked streaky bacon, diced
2 cloves garlic, chopped
1 large carrot, chopped
2 sticks of celery, diced (small pieces)
1 cup of red wine
500 ml of beef stock
50 g of flour to coat the beef
Olive oil – a glug!
Salt and pepper

Hot water crust pastry

450 g plain flour
100 g strong white bread flour
75 g unsalted butter, ½ inch diced
½ tsp salt
100 g lard
2 eggs (using yolks only)

1 x 20 cm loose bottom cake tin
Casserole pot

Method

Flour the diced shin in a bowl and fry on medium heat in a little oil in a large pan until lightly brown.

Add a little oil to a casserole pot, then add the beef, frying gently.

Put the onion, carrot, garlic, celery and bacon into the frying pan and cook until lightly coloured. Season and transfer to the casserole pot. Add the wine and stock.

Cook in the oven at 200 degrees C (180 degrees fan) Gas mark 6 for 1 ½ hrs.

The beef needs to 'soften' so allow time to cool.

Pastry

Preheat the oven to 200C (180C Fan) Gas Mark 6. Grease the cake tin lightly with lard

Combine the flour and salt in a bowl, adding the butter. Rub lightly until all combined.

Heat 250 ml of water and the lard in a saucepan to just boiling and the lard has all melted.

Pour this into the flour and mix with a spoon. When cool enough to handle, knead to a smooth dough on a floured surface. Work quickly, as the pastry dries and crumbles.

Set aside one-third of the pastry for the lid and roll out the other two-thirds on a floured board.

Drape the pastry over the rolling pin then loosely lie it over the tin. Using your knuckles, edge the pastry into the tin letting it overlap the edges. Then, roll the rolling pin over the top of the tin for a neat edge. Spoon beef into the pastry and press down to level. Brush the top of the pastry with beaten egg.

Roll out the pastry lid and lay it over the dish, 'crimping' the edge, joining the base to the top.

Place pastry trimmings on the top – decorate as you choose.

Cook the pie at 200C (180C Fan) Gas Mark 6 for 45 minutes. Turn down to 170C (150C Fan) for 30 min. Gas Mark 3

Serve with creamy mash and purple sprouting broccoli.

Terry's Apple Tart

Recipe:

½ kg Braeburn apples for puree
¾ kg Braeburn apples for the top (or any sweet, eating apples)

100 g castor sugar – plus a little for sprinkling
A block of puff pastry
150 g of apricot jam

Method:

Thinly slice the apples for the puree and place them in a saucepan with 75 grams of sugar and 2 tablespoons of water. Cook until soft, then mash into a puree, leaving to cool.

Roll out the pastry and line a flan dish with it, pricking it with a fork. Then spread the puree until the base of the pastry is completely covered.

Peel and core the apples for the top, then thinly slice them, arranging them all over the base, slightly overlapping. Sprinkle with the remaining sugar.

Baking at 200C (180C Fan) Gas Mark 6 for approximately 30 minutes until the pastry is cooked and the apples are browning.

Place the apricot jam in a small saucepan, then add approximately two teaspoons of water.

Warm the jam and water on a gentle heat until well mixed and warm. Then brush the top of the tart with the jam.

Serve with fresh cream or ice cream.

Me, aged 14, with Mum

An appreciative customer –

'To Dear Terry,

'SIMPLY THE BEST'!! comes to mind, thinking about the amazing contribution you have made over the years.

Always ready with a smile and a warm welcome when both Jonny and I have popped in and have always given us time and kindness.

I don't think there are many left of those of the sheer professional standard that you have in spades, you are a true gentleman.

You've set the 'bar' very high and extremely large shoes to fill!

Jonny says to enjoy your fishing, we both hope that you enjoy your retirement to the full. We still miss you very much.

All our good wishes to you both

Bev and Jonny xxx'

Terry Colby

I have known Terry now for a few years, Professionally as the Manager of Wallingford Butchers and as a friend.

Terry at work

Terry is a pleasure to work alongside, takes his job very seriously and I've never met anyone so passionate about their work. He cares continuously about the shop looking the best it can and making sure the Quality of the produce is at its best. His enthusiasm for fresh ideas and approaching new business is a joy to see. Its very rare these days to find someone who loves their job so much and is so professional in what they do. Terry has made Wallingford shop his own creation and you know he has succeeded when you continuously hear praises and people talk about how much they love to shop there.

Terry & his staff

Where do I start? Terry is a very well respected man by everyone who knows him, works alongside him and by each of his customers. He has a great relationship with Steve & Ben who work alongside him in the shop, he treats them with respect and the friendship they have built between the three of them in and out of work is very special.

He He He ....Sorry Boys!!!

Anyway, whichever way you look at it , it's a good solid base for a working team.

Terry is a very loyal person, a sort of old fashioned gentleman who carries his loyalties, his general everyday manners and respect for everyone very high. He is a very kind man and will put himself out to help anyone , a real pleasure to know.

Thankyou for all your hard work and continued support Terry..........Your only 60 anyway, you've got another 60 working years left in you let !!!!!!!!

Epilogue

So where will it take me now?

For a long time, I have thought about Argentina, famous for its beef cattle. I would like to go to Buenos Aires and sample a good steakhouse, not just for the great food, but to experience the ambiance and their culture. Maybe even sample a market there.

Jeannette's ancestors were from Scotland, so we really should do a foodie tour there. I would like to impress Jeannette with its beauty and the friendliness of its people; perhaps rekindle their relationship, and sample some wonderful seafood, Isle of Skye here we come!

There are so many countries I would like to visit, including their markets; maybe a book detailing markets in Europe could be my next project. Bologna, Florence, and Sienna are on the list, as is Spain.

Closer to home I would like to explore home curing, as my salt beef was great, as was my pancetta, and bresaolo could be next. Plenty to see and do, and never a dull moment!

About the Author

Terry lives with his wife Jeannette in Henley-on-Thames.

He has a large family; three children, Alex, Rebecca, and Joanna, and three stepchildren, Sergio, Mario, and Bianca, plus eight grandchildren, all keeping him company.

Terry is a lover of good quality food from near and far, who enjoys and champions locally sourced foods, along with those from around the country and from abroad. He has many followers, who learn much from his skills and knowledge.

He's a very traditional Englishman, and a sports fanatic, having represented his country as a Billiards International. He continues to play snooker and billiards in the local league, of which he is chairman and has been involved in providing tutoring for new, keen players.

A keen gardener and enjoys growing his vegetables.

He loves the outdoors, and with his wife Jeannette, takes their little Maltese dog for a walk.

Terry has a great knowledge of birdlife and enjoys fishing when time allows.

Acknowledgements

This book would never have come to fruition without me being cajoled by my wife Jeannette, continually giving me a 'kick up the backside' figuratively speaking! It was often needed, but she is my biggest supporter, the love of my life, and my best friend.

The man with a vision behind the transformation of Gabriel Machin, Colin Marett, who had a great passion; taking it from its humble beginnings to the fine food shop it's become, who I had the pleasure of working for (and with) for well over 30 years and giving me some freedom to play a part in that evolution.

The Higgs Group, via The Henley Standard, wrote some excellent articles about us all and provided some photographs for inclusion in this book.

The suppliers and producers I encountered during my time in all the places I've worked have all contributed to my journey.

Barry Wagner, for the humorous moments and the opportunity to finish my final days at work, back at the business where it started.

Chris Bubb, for the excellent illustration of the smokehouse, and Vicki Laskey for the invaluable help with proofreading and publication.

Last but certainly not least, all the customers I've had the pleasure of meeting during the execution of my work; we conversed, laughed, and occasionally commiserated together - you all had such an impact on my life.

Printed in Great Britain
by Amazon